THE NETHERLANDS REFORMED CHURCH, 1571-2005

THE HISTORICAL SERIES OF THE REFORMED CHURCH IN AMERICA,
NO. 51

THE NETHERLANDS REFORMED CHURCH, 1571-2005

Karel Blei

Translated by
Allan J. Janssen

WILLIAM B. EERDMANS PUBLISHING COMPANY
Grand Rapids, MI / Cambridge, U. K.

Wm. B. Eerdmans Publishing Co.
255 Jefferson Ave. S. E., Grand Rapids, Michigan 49503/
P.O. Box 163, Cambridge, CB3 9PU U.K.
www.eerdmans.com

Printed in the United States of America

Cover photos:

> upper left, Dom Toren, Utrecht;
> middle right, Domkerk;
> middle left, Nieuwekerk, Den Haag;
> bottom, left to right: Seminary chapel, Hydepark, Driebergen; St.
> Thomaskerk, Aelst.

All photos by Donald J. Bruggink

To those whose Christian ancestry
is in the *Nederlandse Hervormde Kerk*
who have gone to America and continued the faith.

The Historical Series of the Reformed Church in America

The series was inaugurated in 1968 by the General Synod of the Reformed Church in America acting through the Commission on History to communicate the church's heritage and collective memory and to reflect on our identity and mission, encouraging historical scholarship which informs both church and academy.

General Editor,
> The Rev. Donald J. Bruggink, Ph.D, D.D.
> Western Theological Seminary
> Van Raalte Institute, Hope College

> Laurie Baron, copy editor
> Russell L. Gasero, production editor

Commission on History
> James Hart Brumm, M.Div., Blooming Grove, New York
> Lynn Japinga, Ph.D., Hope College, Holland, Michigan
> Mary L. Kansfield, M.A., New Brunswick, New Jersey
> Melody Meeter, M.Div., Brooklyn, New York
> Jesus Serrano, B.A., Norwalk, California
> Jeffrey Tyler, Ph.D., Hope College, Holland, Michigan

Contents

Introduction to the English Edition

This book originated as part of a series of books intended to introduce the Dutch public to Christian denominations, world religions, and other religious groupings present in the Netherlands. That it needs to introduce the Reformed to a country that was forged in a period when national independence was so deeply interwoven with the Reformation of the church, and that as a "Reformed" Reformation, may seem a bit strange, and is perhaps telling. Nevertheless, there are a number of reasons why students of the Reformed tradition will welcome this small book by Karel Blei, recently retired general secretary of the Netherlands Reformed Church.

I

First, there exists no history of that church in English since Maurice Hansen's readable but dated book, published in 1884. The date itself is significant, for it indicates that Hansen's story takes the reader through the *Afscheiding* of 1834, an event of major importance to the American Reformed churches of Dutch origin. However, the book perforce cannot tell the story of the later major division, the *Doleantie* (in 1886), nor can it describe the emergence of a lively but divisive set of theological schools that shaped the life and religious outlook of local congregations. For the same reason it could not relate the remarkable story of the renewal of the Netherlands Reformed Church in the middle of the twentieth century. Blei makes the full story available to English readers briefly, but completely, for the first time.

II

Second, the story relates a number of central threads in the story of the Reformed Church in America (RCA)—with significant relevance to the Christian Reformed Church as well. The Netherlands Reformed Church (or *NHK*) *was* the Reformed Church in America in its early centuries. It wasn't until 1771 that the Articles of Union were adopted that began the process of independence from the mother church. Until that time, the American church had been under the auspices of the Classis of Amsterdam. Thus, the story of the *NHK* as it emerged within the Reformation and found its early high point at the Synod of Dort, is the story of the RCA.

The story of the formation of the Dutch church is the story that shaped and continues to shape the RCA. The first synod, at Emden, laid foundations for a church order that would come to an early shape in the *Postacta* of Dort (decisions made after the international delegates returned home in 1619), that in turn set out outlines for a church order still in use in the RCA. The shape of belief and piety articulated in the Heidelberg Catechism, in the Belgic Confession, and in the Canons of the Synod of Dort formed a way of living and believing in the RCA throughout its history. We even retain a liturgical life from that time; the "charge to the minister" in contemporary installation services can be found in the liturgy written at Dort!

Much of this history is available in a number of formats in English. It is instructive, however, to hear the story told with Dutch readers as the primary audience, for theological developments in the Netherlands would have a direct influence in the new country. The emergence of the *nadere Reformatie* (the "further Reformation") would make possible American contact with the Great Awakenings and the evangelical culture that was to ensue.

Furthermore, the *Afscheiding* (or "Separation") of 1834 began a chain of events that led to the immigration of a number of Dutch to the United States. Under the leadership of Albertus Van Raalte, they settled on the Black River near what is now Holland, Michigan; following Hendrik Scholte, others found their way to Pella, Iowa. And still others moved on to northwest Iowa. This new immigration would not only mean an eventual increase in churches and membership in the American church. It would also work a theological influence, as the immigrants would emphasize the confessional loyalty that had engaged the Separatists in the Netherlands and would seek it in their new country.[1] The American Reformed church has struggled with this tension in a variety of ways up to the present day. This history locates the American story within its Dutch context.

While immigrants continued to enter the United States in the years that followed, it appears that the two churches went their separate ways. However, the story of the Dutch church would again influence the American Reformed churches (now cousins) in the mid-twentieth century. Leaders in the RCA were interested observers as the Dutch church underwent a renewal following the Second World War (more on that below). The Americans not only followed the emergence of liturgical renewal, the shape of a new church order, or the attempts at a new Reformed confession; they incorporated Dutch insights into their own liturgical renewal, into debates on the nature of office in the church, and even in the attempt to articulate a new confession, *Our Song of Hope*.[2]

III

Third, the further events of the late nineteenth and twentieth centuries themselves make a fascinating chapter in church history, as well as Reformed church history. The aforementioned *Doleantie* (or "Sorrowing") continues the story of the struggle in the Dutch church in the nineteenth century. And it introduces the remarkable figure of Abraham Kuyper, himself an important figure in the Reformed story, and Philippus Jacobus Hoedemaker, a lesser-known figure, but arguably as important. Kuyper became well known in the United States, particularly for his Stone Lectures at Princeton University, in 1898.[3] Among other reasons, these lectures are of significance because they communicated to the United States what "Dutch Reformed" was all

---

[1] The roots of the separation are explored more fully in Gerrit ten Zythoff, *Sources of Secession: The Netherlands Reformed Church on the Eve of the Dutch American Immigration to the Midwest* (Grand Rapids: Eerdmans, 1987), and Elton J. Bruins and Robert Swieringa, *Family Quarrels*, Historical Series of the Reformed Church in America (Grand Rapids: Eerdmans, 1999).

[2] This translator, for example, has in his possession any number of Dutch books of this era from the libraries of leaders like Howard Hageman and James Eelman. On the offices see, Gerrit T. Vander Lugt, "The Offices and the Ordination of Women," in *Proposed Revision of the Constitution and Report on the Ordination of Women* (Office of the Stated Clerk: June, 1957), 63-75. New Brunswick Theological Seminary published a translation of *Fundamenten en Perspectieven* in 1955.

about. Unfortunately, despite Kuyper's unarguable genius and insight as an interpreter of the Dutch Reformed tradition, it was from the perspective of the minority church (albeit one that claimed to be the true continuation of the genuine Reformed history). Kuyper continues to be an important figure for many in the American Dutch Reformed family.

Hoedemaker is less well known, and for understandable reasons. He was a difficult thinker, and often a difficult person. However, his understanding of the church as a church for the entire people and nation of the Netherlands was to prevail. In fact, not only the church order that emerged after the Second World War, shaped as it was by the notion of apostolicity, but the church order of the merging church, *Samen op Weg*, reflects Hoedemaker's theological and ecclesiastical commitments.

The story of how the *NHK* found its way through its differences to the new church order, that in itself codified a new way of being church, is in itself a good tale. By the 1930s, the church had reached an impasse. In the words of the well-known missiologist, Hendrik Kraemer, it had become a "hotel church." There was room for everyone. But all stayed in their own rooms. Peace could be maintained so long as no one bothered anyone else. Blei relates how during the war that impasse was broken, and he details the remarkable results that ensued. The story is telling for fellow Reformed Christians as we observe how a sister body found her way ahead.

The story continues. It was during the preparation of this English edition that the slow but steady process of church union in the Netherlands reached its goal of becoming one church. Blei was himself a central player in the process and so is uniquely positioned to relate this story. In fact, he graciously revised the original Dutch edition to reflect the latest events. He allows us to be spectators at an exciting moment in the history of the church.

IV

Fourth, this little book relates more than a history. Blei reflects on the *identity* of the *NHK*. What does it mean to be Reformed in a

---

3   Published as *Lectures on Calvinism* (Grand Rapids: Eerdmans, 1931). On Kuyper, see James D. Bratt, *Dutch Calvinism in America: A History of a Conservative Subculture* (Grand Rapids: Eerdmans, 1984), 14-33.

secularized culture? What does it mean to be loyal to confessions that date from the sixteenth and seventeenth centuries? And what does it mean to live in a society that is shaped by Reformation principles, even as the number of church members has dipped to its lowest number? We listen to such reflections from the other side of the ocean. But we listen with eager ears; and although our circumstances differ, they are our questions as well.

A number of years ago, I found myself in a Dutch Reformed congregation on a Sunday morning. It was a curious moment. On the one hand, I felt oddly comfortable for one for whom the Dutch language was still almost totally foreign. I felt as if I was not far from the church in which I was raised. The hymns and the sermon were in the right places. How people sat, and where, what they sang, and when, the coffee hour that followed the service, the catechism question in the bulletin—it all could have been in central Iowa. But of course it wasn't home; it was also quite strange.

Something of that sense meets the Reformed reader of Blei's book. In Barbara Tuchman's trenchant phrase, we see ourselves through a "distant mirror." For example, Blei's recurrent theme of the *NHK* as a *volkskerk* gives fresh meaning to Article 36 of the Belgic Confession on the relation between the church and the governing authority. The American church not only lives with a separation of church and state, but also celebrated it in the Preface to the Explanatory Articles,[4] and so must reflect differently on that article. Nonetheless, in this mirror one is given to see something of the nature of the RCA, as well as to begin to catch its contours as distinct from other American Reformed bodies.

Furthermore, Blei gives us a picture of an alternative history—the way the America church might have gone. Here is how a church that struggles to remain faithful to Scripture, to find a place for the same confessions, to live under a similar church order, does its business. It isn't how the American church developed. But it is how a Reformed church did find its way into the present, the church from which the RCA emerged in the early days of the American experience.

Furthermore, readers can be particularly grateful, for Blei is himself an interesting and extremely well informed guide. He served as a pastor in the church prior to his appointment as general secretary. He is also a theologian of significant accomplishments, publishing on

---

[4] See Daniel J. Meeter, *Meeting Each Other in Doctrine, Liturgy & Government* (Grand Rapids:Eerdmans, 1993), 48-50.

theological, historical, and ecclesiastical issues in the Netherlands. More broadly, he has served on the Central Committee of the World Council of Churches. This series, and its readers, are in his debt.

Allan Janssen
Summer, 2005

Preface

This book was published in Dutch, in 2000. I am happy that an English translation now is ready to appear. Important new developments in Dutch Church life have taken place in the five years following its original publication. For that reason the text could not be reedited simply in its original form. Hence an update was necessary, particularly in the concluding chapters. I hope this book in its present form will be for the American reader a faithful introduction to the Netherlands Reformed Church, both to its fascinating history and to its present reality.

I would like to express here a special word of acknowledgment to the Rev. Dr. Allan J. Janssen, who provided for the translation into an English without any "Dutchisms" and who also added explanatory notes and a more specific introduction for American students of the Reformed tradition.

Karel Blei
June 2005

CHAPTER 1

Introduction

"Do we believe in the same God?" So reads the challenging title of a book that appeared a few years ago that surveyed the situation of the Netherlands Reformed Church.

Four authors wrote on the situation, all Reformed, each coming from different sectors of this church. The differences in their evaluation of the situation in the Reformed Church are striking, and the outsider finds him or herself confronted with the question: What really keeps the Reformed together? Why do they all remain members of one and the same (national) church? Do they believe in the same God?

The question is unanswerable, and not only for outsiders. Netherlands Reformed people themselves have no answer. The preaching and the spiritual climate in the local Reformed congregations can differ broadly among themselves. How can it be that all the differing congregations still belong to the one Netherlands[1] Reformed Church?

One attempting to sketch this church most likely considers such descriptions as: broad, vague, less representative of a particular belief perspective than it is inclusive of a number of spiritual streams.

---

[1]   It is important to note that the name of the church, in Dutch, is *Nederlandse*. In this work, that word will be translated as "Netherlands." However, in Dutch, *Nederlands* would mean the "Dutch" Reformed Church, with nuances that the Dutch name wishes to avoid. The church is the church of the nation, the Netherlands, and not a "Dutch" church, in the sense that it is the Reformed Church of a Dutch variety.

1

Volkskerk

Sociologically, a distinction can be made between two types of church: the *volkskerk*[2] and the "free church."

A *volkskerk* is characterized by breadth and plurality. It coincides with a particular *volk*, or at least understands itself especially responsible for and related to the whole of the people. Members of the *volk* also count (more or less) self-evidently as members of this church. The "people's church" is the established, official church of the nation. As such it has, from the perspective of the state, particular privileges in public life. It is seen—or at least views itself—more as the leading representative of what is particular to the nation than as the representative of a particular, well-defined faith perspective.

Over and against the type *volkskerk* stands that of the "free church." It includes at most only a minority of the population. One becomes a member of this church not by birth, not as a matter of course, but by choice, by one's own decision. It neither claims nor desires special privileges in public life but insists on its own freedom over and against the government. It is characterized by the strength of the faith convictions of its members, a strength that can tolerate no plurality.

Neither of these two types can be found in a pure form any longer. The most one can say of a particular church is that it approximates one type more than the other. In this case, it can be said of the Netherlands Reformed Church that it—more than any other Dutch church body—is related to the type *volkskerk*. That is clear already from its name ("Netherlands").

That name came into use officially at the beginning of the nineteenth century. Prior to that time one spoke of the Reformed Church in the Netherlands,[3] which indicates that it could not completely fit with the type *volkskerk*. In reality it has never included

---

2   Literally "people's church." However, "people" is understood as roughly the population of the nation.

3   It is difficult for the English speaker to keep the names of the Reformed church straight. The words *Hervormde* and *Gereformeerde* both mean "Reformed." The confusion will become all the greater as the words are sometimes used interchangeably. However, later Reformed churches, particularly in the nineteenth century, consciously took the name *Gereformeerde* for their own communion. This usage is connected to the fact that *Gereformeerde* often pointed to an older understanding of the church, one that was faithful to the church of the Reformation, at least to

the entire population of the Netherlands. Furthermore, membership in this church was never simply automatic. Still, it was the privileged church during two centuries of the Republic of the United Netherlands, and it was related to the existing order in a particular way. That it did not so much represent one particular point of belief as it embraced a great divergence of spiritual streams is connected with its character as a *volkskerk*.

Around 1800, the privileged position of the Netherlands Reformed Church came to an end. The principle of separation of church and state was introduced. But a notion of its particular relationship to the whole of the people of the Netherlands remains in this church. After the Second World War the notion of the *volkskerk* was reintroduced into the language, in particular Reformed theological circles, but with a new, missionary overtone: it no longer meant as much "church *of* the *volk*, as much as, "church *for* the *volk*." The Netherlands Reformed Church consciously intended to be the church in the midst of the society. That endeavor characterizes the church into the present, although the current societal situation forces the church to review the question of what that might mean concretely.

Membership Statistics of the Netherlands Reformed Church

At the beginning of the twentieth century the Netherlands Reformed Church remained by far the church with the largest membership. According to the census of 1899, the church included nearly half—48 percent—of the population of the Netherlands.

Since then that proportion has been considerably eroded. The census of 1947 offered a Netherlands Reformed percentage of 31. Reduction continued at a fast pace, primarily after 1960. According to an estimate and a study based on facts from the Central Bureau for Statistics, in 1990 the percentage of Netherlands Reformed had fallen to 17.

By its own statistics, the Netherlands Reformed Church consisted of 2,133,873 members on January 1, 1998. Of a total population of nearly 15.7 million in the Netherlands, that represents about 13 percent.

The Netherlands Reformed Church is still the largest Protestant

those who used the word to identify with that older understanding. This translation will not translate *Gereformeerde* except in those instances when the context indicates clearly that it is being used to mean "Reformed" in a broader sense.

church in the Netherlands. The number registered as Netherlands Reformed is exceeded only by the number of Roman Catholics. The Roman Catholic Church in the Netherlands also has decreased in membership since 1960—albeit by a smaller measure. At the same time, not surprisingly, the percentage of unchurched has risen dramatically. In 1899, they made up only 3 percent of the population; in 1947 that had already risen to 17 percent. In 1999 nearly two-thirds—63 percent—of the population of the Netherlands viewed themselves as belonging to no particular church.

Causes of Secularization

The process of "dechurchification" (or, "secularization") affects all churches. But none has been affected as much as the Netherlands Reformed Church. That fact provides the occasion, in a book about that church, to examine this matter somewhat further.

Much has been written about the causes of secularization. The report published by the Office for Social and Cultural Planning in 1994, *Secularisatie in Nederland, 1966-1991*, named several important factors. One is the growth of natural sciences and technology, which in turn led to what is called a general trend of rationalization and commercialization. Humans appear to be able to save themselves and need no longer rely on God's help. Above all, the growth in the welfare state renders an appeal for ecclesiastical assistance unnecessary; that further highlighted the fact that the position of the churches has been undermined. All in all, the churches and their doctrines have become unworthy of belief and, for many, superfluous. And as indifference or active rejection of belief grows, more and more parents will refrain from raising their children in the church. That means that the tendency toward secularization is self-reinforcing.

For the Netherlands (which leads the way in this trend in Western Europe) the report cited above points out yet another particular condition. The strong ecclesiastical tie in the Netherlands in the first decades of the twentieth century was the result of emancipating group processes. At the end of the nineteenth century, the Roman Catholic as well as the Reformed (*Gereformeerden*, separated from the Netherlands Reformed Church) had developed significant group identities. A notion of group solidarity (along with the accompanying social control) was deemed necessary to be able to wage the struggle for equal rights with success. So there originated, in the Netherlands more than in any other Western European country, "pillarization," that shaped not only the life of faith but also societal life. In reaction, other groups as well, in specifically Reformed circles, for example, formed "pillars." Broadly, the conviction reigned that one belonged first to a particular portion of the people (as "pillar") and only subsequently to the people of the Netherlands as a whole. The diverse church groups that were involved in this "pillarization" were well-knit communions that could function as bulwarks in the struggle for emancipation.

However, the emancipation process appeared completed by about 1960. Roman Catholics and the Reformed (*Gereformeerden*) no longer held to the notion that the society had put them at the disadvantage. The necessity of a strong group identity was no longer felt. Indeed, group identity was experienced as oppressive in many ways and in a growing measure. It has been superseded, in part as consequence of the influence of the media of mass communications: television screens do not respect the borders of a "pillar"; they force themselves into every home. One turned away from "pillar" thinking; and where the church had represented the "pillar" par excellence, one turned away from the church as well.

That process happened all the more thoroughly—and over the entire population of the Netherlands—as prosperity increased. A mentality developed that was strikingly imaged in the popularity of the supermarket: rather than waiting in the shop at the counter until (finally) it is one's turn to be helped, one walks along the shelves with one's own shopping cart and helps oneself. That is characteristic of the ruling behavior in contemporary society. And that metaphor applies as well on the level of norms and values. A trend toward individualization rules. Tradition and traditional values are no longer received and accepted as self-evident. One "shops," and fills one's own cart from a wide offering of world views. Each puts together his own spiritual package, his own "life view." A particular church connection is no longer necessary.

Confessing Members, Baptized Members, and Birth Members

Something more must be said about the membership statistics of the Netherlands Reformed Church. In Article II of its church order, three types of members are distinguished: confessing members, baptized members, and birth members.

"Confessing members" are those who have made public confession and thereby have become members with full rights. They are those who have also chosen church membership and have accepted responsibility for it.

"Baptized members" are those who were baptized as children—on request of their parents—but have not (yet) made public confessions by their own formal choice and decision. This category includes children and adults. Adults as well can thus be members of the church, without having chosen it themselves.

Most remarkable is the category, "birth members." The term is not official but in practice is very established and is clear in its meaning. The church order describes them as "those who are born to Reformed parents." It is thus about people who not only have made no public confession, but who also are not baptized. By virtue of the fact that their parents are Reformed, they are counted as "belonging to the Netherlands Reformed Church."

This concerns children as well as adults. No age limit applies for those "belonging to the Netherlands Reformed Church" on the basis of "birth to Netherlands Reformed parents." Indeed what are "Netherlands Reformed parents"? They can be (or have been) confessing members or baptized members or even themselves birth members. In the last case church membership depends on the link by birth, not only of those immediately related but also of one's parents (or of preceding generations).

Only the Netherlands Reformed Church has this category of church membership. None of the other churches understand church membership by virtue of birth. Thus, none of the other churches so nearly approaches, in their self-understanding, the type *volkskerk*.

Church Membership and the Covenant of Grace

It is true that church membership and citizenship in the Netherlands is not simply identified in the article of the church order cited. "Birth to Reformed parents," according to Reformed church order, does not make one a Reformed Church member in the same way as birth to Dutch parents makes someone a citizen of the Netherlands. The Reformed church order makes an important note in this matter: whoever belongs to the Netherlands Reformed Church belongs "by virtue of the covenant of grace."

Thus, at a foundational point of a practical regulation on church membership, an appeal is made to an understanding of belief derived from the Bible: God's covenant. In the Old Testament the covenant of God with the people of Israel is articulated, a covenant that embraces all generations of that people and so remains in effect "from generation to generation." In the New Testament this covenant is articulated in connection with Jesus Christ. This covenant, so goes this way of thinking, is now also valid for the Christian congregation, the church. As in Israel, so in the church the covenant is valid "from generation to generation"; it includes parents and children.

The Netherlands Reformed Church intends to maintain its regulations concerning church membership in conformity with this understanding. With the formulation in the church order that persons are church members "by virtue of the covenant of grace," the church expresses the fact that, at the deepest level, persons (this applies as well for confessing members and baptized members) belong to the church not because they have chosen so for themselves but because God has chosen for them (his people). The church is not so much a human union whereby one can become a member by free decision. It is something peculiar to itself. Thus the borders cannot be sharply drawn. Seen in this way, it is difficult to distinguish precisely between those who do and who do not belong to the church. Persons who have not (yet) asked to become church members still are counted in the church based on the belief that God reckons these humans to his church.

This certainly does not mean that every Dutch person who, so as far as is known, has had Netherlands Reformed forebears would be registered as Netherlands Reformed. The registration is ended when someone (by virtue of his or her express declaration) has made it clear that he or she sets no value on it. No one is or remains registered against his or her will. But there remain people who are registered who are not aware of it.

That is not the intention. As far as possible, the church makes contact with such people, and they are asked about "belonging to the (Netherlands Reformed) church." Often (not always) that comes as a surprise for those asked or even results in protest and the wish (or demand!) to be removed from the register.

A particular action took place in 1990. In the course of that year, all the registered were methodically, in writing, reminded that (or informed that) they were registered. This was necessary in connection with a new plan of membership registration. By virtue of legalities regarding the protection of privacy, the registration of someone's personal facts without her or his knowledge is formally forbidden. Those notified were given the occasion, prior to a particular date, to make known their reservations against being registered. Many made use of the opportunity and were accordingly removed.

Growing Consciousness of Church Membership

Understandably, the decline in membership statistics played itself out primarily among the birth members. In the period 1990-1998 the total number of Netherlands Reformed has declined by 19 percent (in 1990 it was still about 2.6 million). But in the category "birth members" (or "others") the decline was by far the greatest: 34 percent. If one omits this category, then a decline for the confessing and the baptized members together resulted in 12 percent.

Of the above-mentioned 2,133,873 people who were registered January 1, 1998, as "Netherlands Reformed," 707,841 were confessing members, 932,680 were baptized members, 493,352 belonging to the category of "birth members" ("others"). The percentage of birth members in the Netherlands Reformed membership statistics came to nearly 29 in 1990. In 1998 it had declined to 23.

It can thus be said that the consciousness of the ecclesiastical relationship of the average registered Netherlands Reformed Church member has increased.

CHAPTER 2

Origin

The origin of the Netherlands Reformed Church lies in the sixteenth-century movement of the Reformation (or Reform of the Church). This movement arose within the Roman Catholic Church.

Martin Luther

There had already been attempts to reform the church. But the Reformation began in earnest with the appearance of Martin Luther (1483-1546). As professor in Wittenberg, through his studies in the New Testament, in particular of Paul's letter to the Romans, he became convinced that the essence of the gospel is the message of the justification of the godless by faith alone. Justification is addressed to humans by God, for the sake of Christ. The human needs only to receive this by faith and to respond in thankfulness. In faith, the Christian is "free and subject to no one."

This conviction brought Luther into a collision with the ecclesiastical hierarchy, in particular with its pretension that it was able (and required) to administer God's grace by priestly means. He resisted strongly the subsequent notion that church folk (the "laity") should be dependent on the hierarchy (the priest, the bishop, the pope) for the reception of God's grace. Over and against that notion he proclaimed the "priesthood of all believers": every believer stands directly before God's face.

It was not Luther's intention to leave the Roman Catholic Church. Indeed, he desired reformation, or renewal, of the church, so that the essence of the gospel would (again) be able to resound within the church. At the outset, he firmly trusted that he could find a hearing, at least with the pope. But in discussion he was forced ever more clearly to the recognition that the real, decisive authority in matters of faith lay elsewhere for him, that it lay in the Bible. Only when one could show that his conviction was in conflict with the biblical witness would he be prepared to recant. When his convictions were officially condemned in 1521, and he was excommunicated, the Reformation could continue in no other way than outside the Roman Catholic Church.

John Calvin

Luther's appearance found an enormous response. Many knew themselves to be addressed by his proclamation, not only in Germany, but also outside that country. In Switzerland kindred spirits appeared, who nonetheless added their own accents. One of them was the French lawyer and theologian, John Calvin (1509-1564). He worked in Geneva.

Even more than Luther, Calvin realized that the human who is justified by faith is also called before God to a new, "holy," way of life. Calvin saw the meaning of life as consisting in the honor and praise of God. In his teaching he thus placed great emphasis on the significance of the Law of God, the Ten Commandments.

Coincidentally he developed a concrete organization of the ecclesiastical community. Leadership came to be founded on a church council,[1] in which, beside preachers, elders and deacons were seated as office bearers. The task of the elders included, in part, home visitation to encourage members of the congregation to live actively as Christians. Deacons were charged in particular with the care of the poor and the sick.

Calvin's insight also had application to public life; it must be lived to the honor of God. He did not hesitate to address the Genevan municipality of his day in this matter and he also kept before it the Ten Commandments, particularly as a guide for political action.

The Reformed

In the Netherlands, then still undivided[2] and under Spanish rule, it was above all Calvin's Reformation ideas that were influential. His

---

[1]   *Kerkraad*. The church council is the functional equivalent of a "consistory" or "session" in Reformed church orders of an American provenance. In the Netherlands they consisted of ministers and elders of the local congregation. Later, deacons were added.

[2]   The provinces of what later became the Netherlands included southern provinces of what later became the country of Belgium.

followers here called themselves "reformed." At the outset they had to suffer persecution. A number of preachers died martyrs' deaths. Through persecution and inquisition the church (the Roman Catholic Church) and the state (the Spanish authorities) worked together. The Reformation meant unrest and division. It was thus important for the political powers quickly to nip divisions in the bud.

That did not succeed, however. The Reformed persisted. Printers produced editions of the Bible and helped spread Reformed ideas. Some fled the country. Thus there originated refugee congregations in cities such as London, Frankfurt, Wesel, Emden, and in areas like the Rhineland and the Paltz. But as well (or as haphazardly) as they could, the Reformed also developed in the Netherlands a particular congregational life in the face of oppression. Thus they were prepared to stand up for their rights. And they did not shrink from calling on the highest authority, that of the king of Spain.

Persecution of Faith

That happened with eloquence in an anonymous "letter to the king," which forms the introduction to a document that since has become well known as the *Dutch Confession of Faith (Confessio Belgica)*.[3] The letter and the document were thrown over the wall of the castle at Doornik, in the present Belgium, on the night of November 1, 1561. It was the intention that they would ultimately come into the hands of the Spanish king, Philip II.

This letter is written in the style of a self-defense against false accusations:

> We are, one says, disobedient rebels, who desire nothing other than to sever all political order, to bring confusion into the world, and not only to free ourselves from your authority and power, but even to tear the scepter from your hand....Yet one may not stop at accusation, it is to be proven....We (witness)...before God and his angels, that we desire nothing more than obedience to the authorities, to live in purity of conscience, to serve God and to reform ourselves according to his Word and holy commandments....We (pray) in our gatherings for the kings and princes of the world and in particular for you, O gracious Lord, and for those whom you have placed in administration and rule

---

[3] Better known in English as the Belgic Confession.

in your districts, nations, and lordships. For we have assuredly learned from God's Word as well as through the continual education of our teachers, that the kings, princes, and authorities have been ordained by God.

Even the tortures and the martyrdoms that the Reformed have undergone (from the side of those "who deck themselves with your name and power"), so the letter continues, have not provoked them to rebellion. The tortures and martyrdoms certainly prove

> that our desire and our disposition is not fleshly. If it would have been about the flesh we would much more easily been able to advocate and persevere without this doctrine....Never in an orderly spirit that has not been blinded and robbed of its senses, will the thought arise...that those will be rivals to the king...who die for the gospel, in which they see written: give to Caesar what is Caesar's and to God what is God's.

In what follows it is pointed out that this obedience to authority does not emerge from opportunism as, for example, on account of "our small number." The number of supporters of the reformed Reformation is certainly not small:

> We assure you, gracious lord, that there are in your Netherlands more than a hundred thousand men who hold and follow the religion of which we now offer to you the Confession; and still is seen with none of them any preparation for rebellion.

Thus the king must certainly know that when he proceeds with persecution of the Reformed, the result will be an enormous bloodbath:

> What a destruction you will bring then among your subjects, what wounds in your people, what tears, sighs, moaning of women, children, comrades and friends. Gracious lord, may the offspring not describe your rule as bloodthirsty and cruel.

However there is more. The persecution also has to do with the faith conviction advocated by the persecuted. Now:

> Because one persecutes us not only as enemies of your throne and of the public matter, but also as enemies of God and his Church, we humbly pray you to assess this according to the Confession of faith that we offer you.

The king will then see acknowledged and confessed in this confession not only the main points of the Christian faith, as included in the early Christian Apostle's Creed, but also the entire doctrine revealed through Christ, as proclaimed by the evangelists and apostles and maintained in the earliest church. Thus:

> From this Confession you will, we hope, perceive that one unjustly calls us renders of unity, rebels and heretics.

Thus the "letter to the king" that was found November 2, 1561, within the walls of the castle Doornik. The present day reader can judge something of the situation of the Reformed in that time.

Those who discovered the documents, government officials from Brussels, immediately initiated an inquiry to establish the identity of the writer. It appeared to be Guido de Bres (1522-1567). De Bres, formerly a glassmaker, had become a preacher. In his vocation as a glassmaker, he had to consult the Bible, and so was won over to the ideas of the Reformation.

Attempts to arrest him did not succeed. A few years later he fell into the hands of the Spanish government troops. On May 31, 1567, his sentence of death by hanging was carried out.

Growing Resistance

During this same period, a spirit of resistance had clearly begun among the Reformed (in a different way than had been claimed in the "letter to the king"). Discontent with the governmental policy of centralization grew in broad circles of the population. This discontent was abetted by economic scarcity and rising prices. Irritation also increased among the nobility, specifically among the noble *stadhouders* (or "governors") from diverse regions. Among them Prince William of Orange (1533-1584), governor of Holland, quickly stepped forward. In 1566 the lords presented a united petition to the overlords that requested an easing of measures against heretics.[4] An answer was late in coming.

[4] The nobility who presented the petition to the king's governess in Brussels, Margaret of Parma, were called *gueux*, or "beggars." The word was transformed into the Dutch word, *geus*, and was proudly worn as a badge that one was a Protestant. This was also the root of the term "Sea Beggars," who became so important in both the struggle for independence and the rise of Protestantism in the Netherlands. See Jonathan Israel, *The Dutch Republic: Its Rise, Greatness, and Fall 1477-1806* (Calrendon: Oxford, 1995).

The Reformed moved ahead all the more audaciously. They began to hold services in public, outside the towns. These drew great interest. Here and there they even demanded the use of a church building (cloister church or parish church).

In that same summer of 1566, general dissatisfaction discharged itself in a wave of destruction directed against Roman Catholic churches and chapels. In a number of places, although not in the important cities, groups forced their way into churches and destroyed images and altars, missals and vestments.

The Reformed church councils did not organize this "iconoclastic fury." They were overtaken by events. But neither did they disapprove.

The Uprising

The ruling power decided to take punitive measures. In 1567 the Duke of Alva arrived as the new governor in the Netherlands in the name of Philip II to put matters firmly in order both politically and ecclesiastically. His punitive expeditions, taken in 1568 (which ushered in what would later be called the "Eighty Years War"), and his high-handed method clearly succeeded well in the short term, but in the longer view led to still greater dissatisfaction, even to rebellion. Naturally, William of Orange[5] took leadership. Indeed, he tried continually to keep Roman Catholics and Protestants together and to unite them in the struggle for freedom.

In 1572 the uprising began to take more concrete forms. Particularly in Holland and Zeeland, a number of cities declared themselves for Orange.

The Reformed were at the forefront of the struggle. The motivation provided by their new faith and their rejection of Roman Catholicism made them the most radical resistors against the Spanish authority. They struggled not only for freedom, but also for the (their Reformed) truth. They were not satisfied to drive out the Spanish troops. They desired more than anything else the opportunity to freely proclaim the gospel. They wanted a reformation (purification) of the existing church, in such a way that an end would be made to all Roman

---

[5]   Orange was originally Roman Catholic. Later he became Lutheran, especially while in Germany hoping to raise money from princes in that area sympathetic to the Reformation. He later became Reformed, but he always maintained a relatively irenic attitude in religious matters, hoping to avoid religious division among the population of the Netherlands.

Catholic ecclesiastical life. And they desired a government that would take sides in church affairs, a government that not only prevents "false preaching," but also prepares a clear path for and makes possible the proclamation of the "true doctrine." It was a struggle in which they could appeal to Calvin's thoughts on the task of the government.

The Synod of Emden, 1571

But as yet no possibility existed within the borders of the Netherlands to establish Reformed ecclesiastical life. There was, of course, still no possibility of holding an official church gathering there that would be overarching and representative of all Reformed local congregations. Such a gathering was necessary for the discussion of a number of questions that had to be decided in common.

Emden, in German East Friesland, was the city where, from October 4-13, 1571, such a gathering assembled for the first time, the first "national synod" of the Reformed Church in the Netherlands. It consisted of preachers (ministers of the Word) and elders, twenty-nine in number, representatives of the congregations in the Netherlands as well as from refugee congregations. The meeting was held intentionally in the week in which the yearly market was also held in Emden, so that those attending be as inconspicuous as possible among other travelers to Emden in the middle of the crush.

This synod drew the outlines of the organization, the structure, of the Reformed Church. The church order that was drawn up included as the first article a fundamental determination that reads:

> No church (i.e., local congregation) shall have precedence or rule over another, no minister over minister, no elder over elder, no deacon over deacon, but rather each will be alert for all suspicion thereof and occasion thereto.

This prescription made clear immediately that the Reformed Church would look completely different from the Roman Catholic Church. Any thought of hierarchy was hereby excluded from the church. In no case might one consider oneself "higher" or "above" another.

On the other hand, this prescription did not intend to leave the question of mutual connection unsettled. It was also prescribed that a general synod should occur every two years. In addition, in the meantime, yearly "provincial synods" must be held for the churches (i.e., congregations) by region: in the German countries, in England,

and "under the cross" in the Netherlands. In each congregation, the church council must gather (at least!) once each week. Furthermore, as a connecting link between the provincial synods and the church councils the "classis" was instituted, a connection of congregations in a particular district (neighboring congregations). The representatives of the congregations (church councils) would be required to gather in classical assemblies once or twice every half year.

It was also decided that preachers and elders would appear together as representatives of their congregations. This was to ensure that preachers would not constitute a majority in ecclesiastical gatherings.

In the structure of the Reformed Church, the classis received a key function. It would represent the general church (the general church connection) to the local congregations, and conversely it represented the local congregations to the general church. Where a congregation desired to call a preacher, it could issue the call with the necessary classical approval. Furthermore, the classis was required to practice discipline over (oversight of) the preachers.

Besides being a complete rejection of hierarchical tendencies, this entire structure of the assemblies was thus intended to maintain the connection between the local congregations and to resist disintegration.

The confessing character of the Reformed Church was also underscored in Emden. One solemnly signed the *Dutch Confession of Faith* (drafted by Guido de Bres), "to prove the unity in doctrine among the churches of the Netherlands": Further prescriptions were written concerning the textbooks used for education in the faith: the *Heidelberg Catechism* for Dutch-speaking congregations and the *Genevan Catechism* (drafted by Calvin) for those that spoke French. An alternate catechism could be used as well, provided that it "agrees with God's Word." Synod members in Emden were more concerned about the content of the confession than its precise formulation.

Emden and the Netherlands Reformed Church

Was the gathering held in Emden really an official "national synod"? That is debatable. Not all participants were formally present as representatives of their congregations. Still, the decisions of Emden have in fact been accepted as valid for the entire church from the outset in the liberated Netherlands. Since Emden, the congregations under the cross together with the refugee congregations in Germany and England formed one church "ingrafted into one body." Thus, the "national synod of Emden" can be viewed as the official beginning of what much later would be called the "Netherlands Reformed Church."

It is true that this church is not the only one in the Netherlands that can appeal to Emden. In the Netherlands, Reformed Protestantism, particularly in the nineteenth century, has been spread broadly over a number of church bodies that all, in one way or another, identify themselves as "Reformed." But as a national church, the Netherlands Reformed Church may still in particular recognize its origin in Emden.

The foundations laid by Emden in the church order are still to be found in the church order of the Netherlands Reformed Church. The structure of this church remains in full agreement with the guidelines given in Emden. The "assemblies"[6] continue to exist, consisting of preachers and other office bearers (elders and deacons), at various levels: local, classis, province, and nation.

The delimitation that opens the church order accepted at Emden—that one church (local congregation) may not rule over another, or the one minister or elder or deacon over others—finds its echo in the Reformed church order (in Article V).[7] The rejection of hierarchical tendencies is even radicalized; the current church order adds the stipulation that "the one office may not dominate another."

The *Dutch Confession of Faith* and the two catechisms of Heidelberg and Geneva are still valid in the Netherlands Reformed Church, as appears from Article X of its church order, where they are confirmed as confessional writings—writings in which the "confession of the fathers" is "included" as guideline for confessing today. Here too, the line of Emden has been carried forward.

On the Way to Political Independence

The beginning of the Reformed Church in the Netherlands virtually coincides with the beginning of the independence of the nation of the Netherlands. The formal proclamation of this independence

6   "Assemblies" translates *ambtelijke vergaderingen,* a phrase that escapes precise English rendering. It is an important phrase in that it indicates that the assemblies are gatherings of office-bearers (those inducted into an *ambt*), usually elders and ministers, although it would later include deacons as well. In the Reformed Church in America, e.g., the assemblies are the consistory, classis, regional synod, and General Synod.

7   Of the *Dutch Confession of Faith.*

from the Spanish king would happen in 1581. But in fact one could see it happening already in 1572, one short year after Emden.

We already mentioned that in that year a number of cities in Holland and Zeeland openly chose the party of William of Orange in his struggle against the Spanish oppression. In July of that same year a gathering of the States of Holland took place in Dordrecht. That did not happen on the initiative of the "legal authority" (the Spanish king), but on the initiative of the cities of Holland that in the meantime had begun to resist this legal authority. Up to this time, governors had always been named by the king. At this gathering, however, William of Orange was chosen to be governor. It was decided to provide him the necessary financial means to go forward in the struggle for freedom.

Clearly, the way to independence had begun its course. A development had been initiated, and there was no turning back.

CHAPTER 3

Public Church

As we have seen in the previous chapter, the Reformed Church in the Netherlands, including the refugee congregations that belonged to it, manifested itself as one church for the first time at the Synod of Emden in 1571. In this chapter we see how this church would soon become the "public church" in the political system of the new Netherlands.

Space Claimed for Reformed Church Services

In the cities that had joined the rebellion since 1572, the Reformed pressed city administrations not only for permission to hold their own church services, but for a prohibition of Roman Catholic worship. The city administrations did not always accede to the demands of the Reformed. In such cases, the Reformed did not hesitate to force themselves inside church buildings and demand them for their own use. That was invariably coupled with "purification"; all that specifically recalled Roman Catholic worship was demolished. An "iconoclastic fury" thus broke out once again, albeit with less violence than in 1566, but with greater precision and with clearer focus.

Accompanying this "purification" was a rearrangement of the space within church buildings. In Roman Catholic worship, the celebration of the "sacrament" (holy action) of the "meal" of bread and wine is most central. No Sunday can pass without the sacrament. Bread and wine are "consecrated" and offered up as the "offering of the Mass," in which the offering of Christ's body and blood on the cross

19

are made present anew. That requires a central place for the "altar," to which and on which this ceremony takes place. For the Reformed, by contrast, what was most important was not the sacrament of bread and wine (or as they called it, "The Lord's Supper")[1] but the interpretation and proclamation of the Bible as God's Word. Thus, the pulpit became the central point, around which churchgoers gathered themselves, originally standing and, later (the sermons were long!), sitting.

They viewed the Lord's Supper as an accompanying sign and seal for the clarification and further confirmation of the proclaimed Word. In their understanding there could be no talk of a (renewed) "offering" of Christ's body and blood. Thus an "altar" was no longer necessary in their church buildings; whatever "altars" remained were removed. A Communion table was necessary, of course; but then only in church services when the Lord's Supper was actively celebrated. That took place at most four to six times a year, and such would remain the rule until the twentieth century in what now is called the "Netherlands Reformed Church."

The 'Alteration' of Amsterdam in 1578

The course of events in Amsterdam is illustrative. This city refrained from the rebellion against Spanish authority longer than any other. Although the States of Holland had chosen for William of Orange, that did not change the mind of the Amsterdam city council. The change ("alteration") took place in 1578, and then through the powerful intervention of the Reformed residents of the city.

On May 24 of that year a church council was chosen by the Reformed. At their first gathering, they marked the official beginning of the local Amsterdam congregation. The same members of the church council appeared at the city hall two days later and demanded the resignation of the city councilors. The councilors were marched off by officials of the militia and placed by ship, literally, "on the dike."[2] A new city council was appointed, with several church councilors among its members. A short time later the Reformed took possession of all the church buildings, and altars and images were removed. An inscription on the choir screen in the Old Church of Amsterdam still stands as a reminder of these events:

[1]   *Avondmaal*, literally, "evening meal."
[2]   This is a play on a Dutch idiom: *aan de dijk zetten* is to give someone the sack, to fire, to discharge. In this case, the metaphorical phrase becomes literal!

The abuse in God's Church gradually introduced
Is now abolished in the year seventy eight

The Reformed did not want to be a "new" church, "along side of" the old Roman Catholic Church. They pretended to be nothing less than the (purified) continuation of the old church. Thus many old, formerly Roman Catholic, church buildings came into the possession of the Reformed in Amsterdam and elsewhere. Many are still property of the local, now Netherlands Reformed, congregations, or at least are used for Netherlands Reformed Church services.

Subordination of Other Faiths

In many places, primarily in Holland and Zeeland, an official ban of Roman Catholic worship was enacted. Local Roman Catholic ecclesiastical property and cloisters were taken over by city authorities. Religious communities were disbanded. Church wealth was used to finance church life and work in local Reformed congregations. Preachers and schoolmasters (as well as religious educators) among others were paid from proceeds received from these properties.

Assuredly, freedom of conscience was allowed for Roman Catholics. In some places the rich privately accommodated priests who could thereby practice pastoral care in the surrounding neighborhood. The control of the authorities over the potential activity of Roman Catholic priests was uneven at best.

Less difficult was the position of the adherents of other faiths, such as Lutherans and Anabaptists, although they were still subordinated to the Reformed. The Lutherans were followers of Martin Luther. The Anabaptists (currently usually called "Mennonites") were characterized principally by their rejection of infant baptism (the custom of receiving children into the congregation by sprinkling them with water) and through their critical stance toward the political system. Their church services were not forbidden, but their church buildings had to remain absolutely inconspicuous and their church services could not be announced by the ringing of bells.

William of Orange, Freedom Fighter

Developments went a completely different direction than William of Orange had hoped. He was devoted to the cause of freedom of conscience and of toleration, of equal rights for both Protestants and Roman Catholics.

On the other hand, he could not continue without the support of the Reformed in his struggle for freedom. Born Lutheran and raised Roman Catholic in the court of the Spanish king in Brussels, he felt himself ever more strongly attracted to the Reformed faith. For him as well, the struggle for freedom was a matter of faith.

This appears strikingly in a letter that he wrote August 9, 1573, to the leaders of the rebellion in North Holland. The situation there had become perilous following a Spanish offensive; Haarlem had been reconquered by Spanish troops and Alkmaar was under siege. The prince was asked: "Is there still hope? Is there a mighty 'potentate' who can come to help as a comrade?" William of Orange wrote in reply:

> That already before we have begun this matter and the protection of Christians and other oppressed in this nation, we made such a firm covenant with the supreme Potentate of Potentates as such, that we are wholly assured, that we and all who firmly trust thereon, shall in the end be freed by his awesome and powerful hand, despite his and our enemies.

These words express the same spirit of trust in God that we know from the *Wilhelmus* (still in use as the Dutch national anthem and as a hymn). This song, originating between 1570 and 1574, comes in the guise of an encouraging word spoken by William of Orange ("*Wilhelmus* of Nassau") to the Dutch people. It was not written by the prince himself but is placed in his mouth. It is nonetheless a striking articulation of the faith that must have shaped the life of William of Orange.

Later in 1573 William openly chose for the Reformed side. At that time, he participated for the first time in a Reformed celebration of the Lord's Supper.

The First National Synod in the Netherlands: Dordrecht, 1578

The formation of Reformed ecclesiastical life was undertaken energetically in the midst of the tensions of the continuing war with its changing fortunes. Church councils were formed. In accordance with the decisions of Emden, 1571, provincial synods took place in various regions; they had to attend to a variety of practical questions.

In 1578 a national synod gathered for a second time, the first on Dutch soil. This time the gathering took place in Dordrecht. Again full consideration was given to the structure of the Reformed Church instituted by the Synod of Emden, with its assemblies on the local, regional (classical), provincial, and national (general) level.

Consideration was given to the specific task of each of the assemblies. The differences in level (from local to national) implied no relationship of authority. One certainly spoke of "lesser" and "greater" gatherings, but "greater" does not mean "higher." Here again, any thought of a possible hierarchy in the church was carefully excluded.

It was formulated as a general principle that "one shall bring no matter to greater gatherings except those that could not be handled in the lesser, or which concern the churches in common." We still find this "principle of subsidiarity" (as it is currently called) in the church order of the Netherlands Reformed Church.

A number of pertinent prescriptions were decided as well, on such questions as Sunday worship, church burials, the establishment of schools, and the establishment of a reading curriculum.

Governmental Involvement in Church Affairs

One specific theme was continually on the agenda of the ecclesiastical gatherings of the time: the relation between the Reformed Church and the "new" government.

The Reformed were completely dependent on the support of the government to finance their church work and congregational life. They addressed the government expressly on this matter. In their confession, the *Dutch Confession*, a passage had already taken up the matter of the vocation of the government. It has, so it says, as its task

> not only to give attention to and to watch over the public order, but also to maintain the holy worship of the church...and to see that the Word of the Gospel is preached everywhere so that God might be honored and served by everyone, as He commands in His Word. (Article 36)

In other words, it is the task of the government to have as its concern that the church (the Reformed Church) be able to do its work.

But how far must the government's concern reach? Would it include control over ecclesiastical matters? That indeed was how the government understood the matter. In any case it was desired that constraint of conscience, now exercised by the Reformed Church and its preachers, be avoided. The government wanted to retain the authority to call Reformed preachers. It also desired a regulation by which elders would be chosen from among and by the city administration.

The government even wanted a decisive vote in matters of doctrinal difference.

Plans to this end were drafted in 1576 by the States of Holland. They ran into sharp resistance from the church. It could see it as nothing less than an intolerable interference. It would mean that the church would become an institution of the state. Church councils would become extensions of the government. Preachers would be under the oversight of the state. That would be completely contrary to the freedom of the Word!

The National Synod of Dordrecht, in 1578, underscored the independence of the church in the calling of preachers and the election of elders and deacons. That also happened in later synodical gatherings. The government could not agree, however, fearful that the church would interfere in matters of state.

In 1586 church and state came to agreement. The national synod held in The Hague that year accepted a revision of the church order in which the desires of the government were more or less met, and which was then received favorably by the government of the various provinces as well. The church retained for itself the right to elect its elders and deacons. It was determined, however, that the city administration could appoint one or two of its members as additional members of the local church council.

In synodical gatherings, the various regional authorities, the Provincial States, could be represented by "political commissioners." They had as their task to ascertain that the synodical gatherings would never make decisions in governmental matters. In practice, these "political commissioners" often intervened forcefully in ecclesiastical matters.

The calling of preachers remained a contested question. The church could not hinder the government from practicing its influence. The course of events differed by province. There was no uniform regulation, applicable for the entire nation, in effect.

Preachers who came into conflict with the local church council on account of their divergent opinions were nonetheless sometimes supported by the city administration and so maintained in their position in the church. In some areas there remained the right to choose preachers by the rich or by the administrators of funds. Elsewhere, in Zeeland for example, the calling of preachers was entrusted to a special, "mixed" commission, half being members of the relevant city administration and half being members of the church council. But certain city administrations refused to accept this regulation because they found it too ecclesiastical.

Public Church

Thus, absolute freedom from state interference was and remained an unattainable ideal for the Reformed Church. That coincided directly with its status as the only officially recognized church: the "public church" in the Dutch political system, a status that it had itself striven to attain.

As "public church," it could not emphasize its own identity in an unlimited way. As such it could not escape its connection with and function on behalf of the whole of the nation. It must thus consider governmental guidelines and desires important for its own life and work. In some matters compromises had to be accepted. We saw just how that was the case in the regulations concerning the calling of preachers and the election of office bearers. It was also the case in other questions, as for example, in the matter of whom may be baptized.

As they had with the Lord's Supper, the Reformed developed their own conception of baptism (the sacrament of sprinkling with water). This conception had been set down in, among other places, the pedagogical "formulary" (decided in 1574) that was required to be read prior to the administration of baptism. They viewed this sacrament as well as a clarifying "sign" and a confirming "seal" to the proclaimed Word. The water indicates cleansing (the washing away of sins) and renewal of life. Whoever is baptized validly belongs to Christ and so is received into the congregation. In contradistinction to the Anabaptists, the Reformed maintained firmly that children, too, could be baptized— but which children?

The principle was clear: it was about "our" children, the children of the true members of the congregation. Children did not as yet understand anything about baptism, or so it was maintained; nevertheless, God's grace in Christ still applied for them. The biblical notion of the covenant already cited in chapter 1 was adduced as further argument. The Old Testament witnesses to the covenant that God has established with Abraham *and* his descendants. Precisely so, the covenant today embraces "us and our children."

The States of Holland, however, had come to a different understanding. In the plans they had framed in 1576, there was no place for a church that would develop into a particular, independent group within the society. The "public church" must be the church of and for all. Thus all children without distinction would have to be baptized.

The National Synod of Dordrecht, in 1578, agreed and in so doing accepted the position of public church. It undergirded that position with a vision in which the breadth and reach of the covenant was underscored. The church of Christ is wider than the Reformed Church. Children of people outside the Reformed Church (such as persons of a sinful way of life, or Roman Catholics) could not, so it was claimed, be refused baptism. How could one ever say that these children fall outside the covenant?

In other areas a close collaboration between government and church emerged. That was the case, for example, with marriages. Marriage had been simply a matter for the government. But the government handed its authority over to the Reformed Church. Preachers thus functioned as "public persons." They appeared as representatives of the government. Even non-Reformed were required to have their marriages confirmed by Reformed preachers. Church buildings functioned as public spaces.

Collaboration also took place in the care of the poor. In some places the administration of funds for the poor or a charitable institution was given over to the deacons by the government. Where that happened, diaconal accounts had to be reviewed for approval by the government. The government also had authority in the election of deacons: government officials chose from the double list that was presented by the church council (following approval by the congregation). In the church's care for the poor, the National Synod of Dordrecht made no distinction between the poor within the church and the poor outside the church: attention must be paid to above all to ascertain the "need of the bereft." The Reformed Church did not limit itself in its activity to its own members. It existed to serve the entire Dutch population.

No 'State Church'

Thus the Reformed Church in the Netherlands became an integral part of the society in several ways. However, that did not mean that it simply became an organ of the state. It was never simply the case that all citizens were members of the Reformed Church, nor was it required of them. Even the government did not intend that. Furthermore, there were matters where the church stood firmly against the government.

That was specifically the case in the admission to the Lord's Table and the practice of ecclesiastical discipline.

As mentioned, the celebration of the Lord's Supper took place four to six times per year. Consequently, the celebrations functioned as particularly significant moments in congregational life. Thus, not just everyone could participate. Admission to the Lord's Table was only open to those who, after receiving education in the faith, had become "confessing members" and as such had been admitted by the church council.

Prior to the celebration of the Lord's Supper, all members who had been admitted were visited at home. This home visitation served to invite each personally to participation in the sacrament. But it also served to ascertain whether there were conditions that made it clear that the person in question could *not* participate. Someone who appeared to hold unchristian notions of the faith or who appeared to live in "scandalous sin" would be able to receive the bread and the wine of the Supper only after evidence of repentance. As long as the person in question remained under ecclesiastical discipline, he or she would be required to refrain from participation at the Lord's Supper. And if that person persisted in unchristian understanding or way of life, he or she would undergo heavier discipline; he or she could even be excluded from the communion of the church.

As with baptismal services, services of the Lord's Supper were preceded by a reading of a pedagogical "formulary" (dating from the same time as the baptismal formulary cited above). It was quite detailed and included, among other things, the "rejection of the unrepentant." The congregation was thereby warned with words from 1 Corinthians 11:29: "Whoever eats and drinks unworthily, eats and drinks judgment to himself."

Meanwhile, the government found this much too stringent. In its plans of 1576, cited above, the States of Holland urged the church to be more flexible and to consider what was practically possible in the matter of admission to the Lord's Table. It was desired that every baptized adult would be admitted to the Lord's Table. A certain oversight of everyone personally would never be possible(?!). Furthermore, the government saw itself particularly authorized to act in matters of discipline. In any case, the government was particularly insistent that ecclesiastical disciplinary measures not be taken except on the authority of the government. Otherwise the danger of double jurisdiction would always exist!

However, the National Synod of Dordrecht, in 1578, held firm to the Reformed conviction that the Lord's Supper is only open to confessing members of the church, who as such are subject to the oversight and discipline of the church. In this case there is surely a peculiar ecclesiastical responsibility that the government cannot transgress.

As stated above, as "public church" the Reformed Church still had not become a "state church." Real, full church membership continued to be bound to specific conditions of personal choice and official admittance. These conditions deterred many. The number of confessing members—the true kernel—remained extremely small in a number of congregations.

Remonstrants and Contraremonstrants

As already stated, it had been determined at the first national synod, in Emden in 1571, that a national ("general") synod must be held every two years.

That intention was not to be realized. Ultimately, that had to do with the political situation. National synods gathered only occasionally and irregularly. The first synod after Emden occurred in 1578, at Dordrecht. The next met in 1581, at Middelburg. The gathering at The Hague in 1586, provisionally, was the last of this kind. The government was no advocate of an all too powerful and self-consciously particular ecclesiastical organization. And the church was dependent on the approval of the government for financial support before it could call together a national synod.

A national synod gathered again in 1618, again at Dordrecht. The occasion was fierce theological and ecclesiastical debates that had originated shortly after 1600 and had in turn led to sharp political conflicts as well. The ruling authority itself had an interest in the matter—that everything be discussed and regulated in a national context. In fact, it was the States-General that called the gathering together and paid for its cost.

The debates mentioned above had to do with the interpretation of a point of faith particularly cherished in the Reformed tradition—the doctrine of election. It was written in the Bible that God has chosen Israel to be his people, with whom he has made covenant. Election set Israel apart as a people, but it includes also a calling to other peoples. It is thus election to salvation *and* to service. In the New Testament God's electing action is also related to the community of Christ, the church.

Along with Israel, it is called a "chosen family" (1 Pet. 2:9). "He has chosen us in Christ before the foundation of the world" (Eph. 1:4).

Calvin had strongly related this biblical discussion of election to the individual person, the believer as solitary individual. Thus he had left in the shadow the aspect of the call to service to others, the (still) non-elect, implied in election. He had focused all thought on the aspect of election-to-(one's own)-salvation. It was his notion that God had already from eternity decided which persons (yet to be born) would receive salvation—and thus, too, which humans would *not*.

Must one then really suppose that God has determinatively rejected (many) humans, already in advance, in a definitive decision? Does this not mean that God is monstrously arbitrary and cruel? Calvin himself also had wrestled with that question. He spoke of a "fearful decision." Still, he had held fast to his conception. Only so could he do justice to what he had read in the Bible, namely, that the salvation of humans is exclusively a graceful act, a gift of grace, from God.

Calvin saw his "doctrine of election" as the strongest conceivable emphasis of the basic conviction of the Reformation, adduced by Luther, that a human is justified before God by grace alone, thus a grace purely received from God, without any deserving from his own side. That not all humans share in this salvation (for not all believe), must revert to God's decision. Is there, logically seen, another conclusion possible?

As has been said, a sharp theological discussion broke out over this matter. Jacobus Arminius (1560-1609), professor at the University of Leiden (established by William of Orange in 1575), had since 1603 emphasized that God can in no way be held responsible for human sin as Arminius interpreted the doctrine of election. In God's relation with humans, God cannot be so all-determinative that no particular responsibility in the matter of belief or unbelief would remain for the human. Certainly God must have known from beforehand, from eternity, who would answer the call of the gospel with (enduring) belief, and who would not. God's decision—again taken from eternity—to elect, to make blessed some, and some not, is then based on "foreknowledge." Those whom God has known would repent and come to belief, *those* then God has also elected.

This interpretation was unacceptable for Arminius's colleague in Leiden, Franciscus Gomarus (1563-1641). Arminius's interpretation meant after all that human salvation is ultimately dependent on one's own faith. How can the human then ever be certain of his salvation?

And most importantly, God's majesty is given short shrift. Gomarus thus maintained that it is not human belief but God's grace that is the ground of human salvation. When humans come to faith, that is also already a gift of grace from God. And God gives the gift to those whom he has decided from eternity to elect. In other words: belief is not a *condition* for election, but a *consequence and characteristic* of being elect. That God has chosen some humans to eternal salvation is not *because* they (as foreseen by God) would come to belief, but *in order that* they (in the extension therefrom) would come to belief.

The discussion grew wider. Arminius himself advocated the calling of a national synod by the government. The synod would have to express itself on the difference. In 1610 (Arminius had then already died), Arminius's supporter, Johannes Wtenbogaert, (1557-1644) along with forty-three others composed a "remonstrance" (declaration) directed to the States of Holland. It was a summary of Arminius's conception and a plea for a revision of the confession of faith. That revision would also have to be discussed in the national synod. In a separate publication, Wtenbogaerdt stated his opinion that the government stood higher than all ecclesiastical gatherings and had the final say in ecclesiastical matters.

A short time later the adherents of Gomarus summarized their understanding in a counter-writing, a "counter-remonstrance." In their judgment, there could be no talk of a review of the confession. They also advocated the independence of the church; the government is not authorized to express itself in ecclesiastical differences in doctrine.

So the "remonstrants" and the "contraremonstrants" came to stand over and against each other as parties in the church. That the government found itself involved in these matters lay in the conditions that were then to hand. Given the differences in understandings set forth by both parties in the matter of the relation between church and state, it is no wonder that the States of Holland and many city councils had sympathy for the remonstrants. The States General, however, were less inclined toward regional—provincial—autonomy, and thus leaned more to the side of the contraremonstrants. The same was true of the governor of Holland, Maurits, the son of William of Orange, as well as with the governor of Friesland, Maurits's nephew, William Lodewijk.

The Synod of Dordrecht, the Canons of Dort

Finally the national synod, requested by both the remonstrants and the contraremonstrants—albeit for different reasons—gathered.

It took place November 13, 1618, at Dordrecht. The synod had an extraordinarily broad composition. It consisted of thirty-seven preachers and nineteen elders, representing various provincial synods. The universities, five in number, were each represented by one professor, who also had the right to vote.

On the invitation of the States General, there were also twenty-six representatives of related churches outside the country: England, various areas in Germany, and Switzerland (French representatives could not come). They could participate in the discussions because they were held in Latin. It is to be noted that the presence of these foreigners gave the synod something of the character of a Western European church council.

The government had a particular interest in this synod. That is clear from the fact that it sent no less than eighteen representatives ("political commissioners").

Only three of delegates to the synod belonged to the party of the remonstrants. Thus there could hardly be a real discussion of the points of difference between the remonstrants and the contraremonstrants. It is true that thirteen prominent representatives of the remonstrants were summoned. But just such "summons" stamped them in advance more as complainers than as partners in the discussion. The remonstrants themselves powerfully resisted the intended procedure and challenged the authority of the synod to bring judgment. This ultimately resulted in their being excluded from the assembly hall by the president, the preacher[3] Johannes Bogerman (1576-1637). A few days later this procedure was approved by governmental decree. The three remonstrant synod members acted in solidarity with their fellow party members and likewise left the gathering.

The substantive discussion of the "remonstrance" consequently took place in the absence of its framers. In refutation of this declaration, a detailed document was proposed. This document was accepted unanimously in April, 1619, and finally, on May 6, 1619, solemnly announced. It has since become well known by the name the Canons (Doctrinal Rules) of Dort.

In separate chapters, the document considered in order: "divine election and rejection," "the death of Christ and salvation through

---

[3]   *Predikant.* Literally, "preacher." However, it denotes what the Reformed Church in America, for example, officially calls a "minister of Word and Sacrament." Hence, this translation will use the shortened term, "minister."

Him," "human depravity and conversion to God," and "the perseverance of the saints." Each chapter was concluded with an express "rejection of errors" in the matter under discussion.

The doctrine of election and rejection comes to summary expression in the following passage:

> That God gives faith to some in time and others not, emerges from his eternal decision...Following this decision, by his gracious council, He softens and bends the hearts of the elect to believe, howsoever hard they may be; but He leaves those who are not chosen to their evil and hardness in his righteous judgment. (I-6)

Of Christ's death on the cross it was said: "it would have been able by itself to reconcile the sins of the whole world, but

> God has willed that Christ, through his blood poured out on the cross would save exclusively those who were chosen from eternity to salvation. (II-8)

The proclamation of the gospel runs into unbelief from some and with others wakens belief and conversion. This last is a gift from God. But the first, so it is said, is the guilt of the human himself; God cannot be reproached for *that*, as if the human were but a passive lump! As to that, God's initiative has not left the humans passive but brings them here into active involvement. Moved by God's power and Spirit, the human, also of herself, indeed, believes:

> God opens the closed heart, He softens what is hard...He...makes the will, that was dead, living; that was evil, good; that not willed, now wills; that was resistant, now becomes obedient. (III-IV, 11 and 12)

The main accent, however, continues to lie with God's powerful initiative. God's own self cares that the "saints," the elect, despite all their sins and relapses, would "persevere" in their belief. It is by virtue of

> the gracious mercy of God that they do not completely lose the faith and the grace or continue to the end in their fall and are lost. (V-8)

A promise that meanwhile—the Canons allow not the least doubt about this—is valid exclusively for the elect, ultimately not for the rejected (with whom, so it is supposed, there can be no talk of genuine belief).

Since their solemn announcement as an official confessional document of the Reformed Church in the Netherlands, the Canons of Dort have been valid as confession along with the Dutch Confession of Faith (from 1561) and the Heidelberg Catechism (from 1563, so-called because it was written by some professors in Heidelberg). These writings are also called the "three formulae of unity."

In July 1619, the synod's decision concerning the Canons of Dort was approved by the States General. Subsequently, the government cooperated in the execution of the disciplinary measures against the preachers of the remonstrant party who refused to resign as preachers. Those to whom the measures applied were banished from the country. Thus the government supported the ecclesiastical disciplinary measures (suspension and deposition from office) with its own measures.

One consequence was that besides the Reformed Church, a new ecclesiastical body, the Remonstrant Brotherhood, originated. At the outset it was heavily persecuted; later it was tolerated.

The Dort Church Order,[4] Continuing Governmental Influence

As with previous synods, the synod also reviewed the church order. That happened at the final sessions, after the foreign representatives had departed. The broad lines of the church order remained unchanged. On the docket were "ministries" (offices) in the church; the task and authority of ecclesiastical assemblies at the various levels (local, regional, provincial, national); confessional matters, the administration of the sacraments and Sunday worship; and oversight and discipline in doctrine and way of life of church members and office bearers.

At the conclusion we find the prescription with which the Synod of Emden in 1571 had begun:

> No church shall have any authority over other churches, no minister over other ministers, no elder or deacon over other elders or deacons. (Article 84)

And the article concerning the various levels of ecclesiastical assemblies was preceded by the prescription that had already been formulated by the Synod of Dordrecht in 1578:

---

[4] The Dort Church Order is particularly important for the Reformed Church in America. Its first church order, The Explanatory Articles, were "explanatory" of the Dort church order. The RCA's church order is still modeled on Dort.

It shall only be enacted in the greater assemblies what has not been able to be considered in the lesser, or that pertains in general to the churches of the greater gathering. (Article 30)

The manner in which this church order, enacted in 1619, reckoned with the interference of the government in ecclesiastical affairs is remarkable.

In the choice of a minister to be called by a church council, it was determined that a consultation ("correspondence") with the local Christian government would be required. And after the choice had taken place, subsequent approval ("approbation") must be given, not only from the members of the congregation, but first from the same government (Article 4).

The right of the government to have one or two of its own representatives in the church council "to listen and to share in deliberation of matters on the agenda" was also confirmed. The governmental representatives would, of course, have to be members (confessing members) of the congregation, as was set forth (Article 37).

The relation to the government was also dealt with in a separate, new article of the church order. The vocation of the government toward the church *and* of the church toward the government was discussed in that article. The first was not new. It had already been discussed in Article 36 of the Dutch Confession. But the real emphasis falls on the second, which was a new element indeed. The vocation of the church toward the government was further described as consisting of two matters. First, there is for "all preachers, elders and deacons," the legitimate requirement

> zealously and faithfully to inculcate on the entire congregation the obedience,
> love and honor that they owe to the magistrates.

As well, they will

> by a becoming respect and correspondence seek to waken and maintain the favor of the government toward the churches.

In this way, so it is stated, concord shall be maintained and that will again be of service to the "well-being of the churches" (Article 28).

Presumably, the synod, with its acceptance of this article, intended to do itself what it called its office bearers finally to do—to placate the government. So it hoped to nudge the government toward approval of this church order. At that point it would be introduced as compulsory for all.

Despite these concessions, the synod's goal was not reached. The States General did not express an opinion. On the other hand, a number of areas officially accepted the church order. Still others (Holland, Zeeland, Friesland, Gronigen) saw no necessity to do so and so retained the old order. In any case it was a situation in which the church must abide greater governmental interference than it preferred. The various sections of the country strongly retained their autonomy, and they didn't want to give it up. The introduction of *one* church order, valid for the entire country, made little sense to them.

Thus the Dort Church Order received the intended legitimacy in only part of the nation. Still, it is an important document. From it one can observe how the synod understood ecclesiastical life to be regulated—and how in many aspects it was in fact regulated. Later, in the nineteenth and twentieth centuries, a number of church events, initiatives, and discussions would in fact revert expressly to this church order.

The State Translation

One more result of the synod's work must be mentioned here. The synod decided to authorize a new translation of the Bible and fulfill a long-cherished desire.

There were, of course, already Bible translations in existence, but the translations were not directly from the original texts. They were always translations of translations. The new Dutch translation would be directly from the original languages, Hebrew and Greek, as "faithful" and as literal as possible. Church members would be able to read the Word of God themselves.

Ultimately, this decision as well was dependent on the agreement and support of the government. It took a few years before the States General made the requisite finances available. The money could be used from the booty of the "Silver Fleet" defeated by Piet Hein.

Translators had already been named by the synod (among them was the synod president Bogerman). In addition, two editors per province were named. The government made it possible that the translators (three for the Old, three for the New Testament) were freed completely from their work (as minister or professor). They were allowed to set themselves up together in Leiden, near the university library there. The work could begin in 1626. The translation was ready in 1635. In 1637 the first printed draft could be offered to the States General. They added a preface in which the publication of the translation was approved and authorized.

The relationship of the government to this translation is also expressed on the title page. The translation came into existence, so it says there, "on the order of the high and mighty lords of the States General"; it is then also, "following the decision of the national synod." This version is the well-known "State Translation."[5]

This Bible translation came into general use and has remained so into the twentieth century. It was read in church services, in schools, and at home in families. For centuries the "State Bible" was the only book in the house. Detailed notes could help the reader understand the text.

The State Translation has had an enormous influence in the formation of the unity of the Dutch language—and therewith has also contributed to the formation of the Netherlands as a nation. Even today there are countless expressions in circulation that derive from this translation, although the speakers are often no (longer) conscious of that fact.

---

[5]   Dutch speakers will know this as the *Statenvertaling.*

CHAPTER 4

Faith and Piety after the Synod of Dordrecht

The national synod held in Dordrecht in 1618-1619 was a high point in the early history of the Reformed Church. With it, the establishment phase of the church came to an end. At the same time it was the beginning of a new phase.

No More National Synods after 1619

The church order enacted by the synod prescribed that a similar (national) synod must be held at least once every three years (Article 50). But as with similar prescriptions of earlier synodical gatherings, this intention was not to be realized. After 1619 no general synod gathered as a whole. In the Dutch Reformed Church, which had been the successor and continuation of the Reformed Church in the Netherlands since 1816, it was not until 1945 that a genuine general synod, constituted by representative office-bearers, was held.

The national government saw no occasion after 1619 for a similar broadly based ecclesiastical assembly at a national level. From their side, the States[1] of the various provinces were too interested in the autonomy of their own areas to desire a full expression of a *unified* national church.

That did not mean that a notion of mutuality among the Reformed across the entire nation did not exist. The three confessional

---

[1] Provincial States were proto-parliamentary gatherings. The "States" represented landed gentry (estates) and were autonomous. The States General was a national gathering of the various provincial States.

writings, including the *Canons of Dort*, were a cohesive factor. That was true as well of the State Translation of the Bible. There were certainly synodical assemblies on the provincial level. And interprovincial contact was maintained. But in any case the accent after Dordrecht, 1618-1619, lay on church life in congregations and regions. Discussions among theologians were held. Spiritual movements manifested themselves in the lives of church members. But a directive or an authoritative word from synod was no longer uttered, indeed *could* no longer be spoken.

Voetius and the Influence of Descartes

With its decision in the doctrinal controversy with the remonstrants, the Dort synod appeared to have brought to an end all uncertainty among the Reformed. The Reformed understanding of the faith had been fully decided and securely safeguarded against all misunderstanding with the acceptance of the Canons. The prescribed course was now to keep this well-built fortress of the faith intact and to defend it against all threats.

It was to that task that Gisbertus Voetius[2] (1589-1676) considered himself to be called, and to which he provided forceful leadership. Voetius was a student and follower of Gomarus. As a young preacher he had participated in the Dort synod. In 1634 he became professor of the recently established "illustrious school"—from 1636, a university—in Utrecht.

Voetius was a theologian who set the agenda. He and his colleagues were concerned with the increasing influence of a new way of thinking introduced by the French thinker Rene Descartes (1596-1650), who lived in the Netherlands after 1629. Descartes maintained that absolute and certain knowledge of reality cannot be found in belief based on authority or on the acceptance of a particular tradition, but only by way of (my own, individual) thinking, reason.

Decidedly, Descartes did not intend thereby to attack or undermine Christian faith. Indeed, he considered that even the existence of God is an absolutely certain conclusion, reachable by

[2] Voetius and Voetian piety was formative for the theology and life of the Reformed Church in America. See Elton M. Eenigenburg, "New York and Holland: Reformed Theology and the Second Dutch Immigration," in James W. Van Hoeven, *Word and World* (Grand Rapids: Eerdmans, 1986), 31-44, where he argues that one reason that the Dutch Reformed immigrants were so readily embraced by the American church was a shared Voetian piety.

means of human thought. The sole fact that the human (himself imperfect, mortal, fallible) can conjecture a representation of "God" as perfect, immortal, truthful and good Essence, said Descartes, cannot be explained other than that this God indeed truly exists: God himself must have implanted this representation. Indeed, the mere thought of the idea of God as "perfect" Essence must logically include the real existence of this God; for how can Someone who does not exist be "perfect"? And that God is "perfect," "true," and "good" must also mean that the world in which I live is real. God has created reality and thus I can be certain of that reality, that my thinking ability and senses do not threaten my perception of reality.[3]

Descartes would exert great influence with this conception. For the first time the human has complete trust in his own rational thought as he investigates reality and truth. The human self stands at the center. Later, in the eighteenth century, one would speak of the "Enlightenment." That movement in fact began with Decartes. Henceforth the development of science would take awesome flight.

Decartes's notions also were to be seen in the Reformed Church. Balthasar Bekker (1634-1698), minister in Amsterdam, would later write a sensational book, *De Betoverde Weereld* [ET, *The Enchanted World*]. In it he combated superstition and witchcraft as well as belief in the real influence of "angels" and "devils." That the Bible clearly talks of such he understood as the accommodation to the belief of the times; he interpreted it as metaphor.

The fortress of Reformed belief, so stoutly defended by the synod held in Dort in 1618 and 1619, appeared to be threatened anew with the emergence of Descartes. Descartes may have intended to offer good, reasoned arguments for belief in God; Voetius considered just that as an attack on the authority of revelation. He desired reasoned thinking as well, but on the *basis* of the accepted belief, not as itself the *foundation* of belief. Thus he was forcefully to combat Descartes's new ideas.

The Further Reformation[4]

Furthermore, Voetius emphasized that purity in doctrine alone was not sufficient. It must be coupled with the inner experience of faith

---

[3]   Readers will recognize this as the Cartesian version of the ontological
      argument for the proof of the existence of God.
[4]   *Nadere Reformatie.* The Further Reformation provides a background for
      the reception of later "evangelical" notions within the American Reformed

and with a way of life consistent with belief. Voetius and his colleagues, among whom was the Middelburg preacher Willem Teellinck (1579-1629), advocated not only for "pure faith," but also for "piety" and for the right "practice of divine salvation."

Mention must be made in this context of the movement of the Further Reformation, a movement that manifested itself powerfully in the seventeenth and eighteenth centuries. The term "Further Reformation" clearly describes the goal. The Reformation as it had resulted from the work of Luther and Calvin must still, so it was held, find its completion in a "further," continuing, reformation, one that not only reaches the head (doctrine), but heart and life as well.

The decisions of the Synod of Dort could relate directly with this movement. We saw that the doctrine of God's eternal decision concerning the election of some and the rejection of others had been laid out firmly in the Canons of Dort. It is no wonder that the question could arise whether and how one could be certain of one's own election.

The Canons themselves had already dealt with this question. The elect receive certainty, it was said

> as they perceive in themselves with spiritual and holy gladness the certain fruits of election which are displayed in God's Word—such as true belief in Christ, a childlike fear of God, sadness according to God's will over sin, hunger and thirst for righteousness, etc. (I-12)

But just that could awaken new, anxious uncertainty. Do I have the fruits within myself? Is what I call my belief genuine faith? Am I sufficiently sorry for (my) sin? Or do I hold out false hopes for myself?

As we saw, faith is centrally described in the Canons as a gift of God. It is God's Spirit, so we heard, who opens the closed human heart and makes the dead will living. Thus the elect come to renewal of life, to "rebirth," to "conversion." It was not denied that the human shares in conversion, but only secondarily. All human activity in conversion and faith is only possible after and by the action of God who has, in God's Spirit, intervened in the human heart.

That gave to the question of certainty of one's own status as elect a more anxious tone. One who is convinced that he can in no way assist

---

family. See Allan J. Janssen, "Reformed and Evangelical: New Questions and Old," in John. W. Coakley, ed., *Concord Makes Strength: Essays in Reformed Ecumenism* (Grand Rapids: Eerdmans, 2002), 115-17.

in his own election longs to be able to glimpse traces of the work of God's Spirit in his own heart. That easily leads to the sigh: "Oh, may it still come to pass..." "Oh, may it also overcome me..."

In this way, the Canons offered humans occasion to concentrate on their own inwardness. This element was strengthened in the movement of the Further Reformation. One reflected on the differing steps that one must go through on the way to perfect certainty of belief. The differing steps became more and more seen as following a fixed sequence, an "order of salvation."

'Convicting' Preaching

Voetius and his followers, the "Voetians," thus began to divide the church-going congregation into differing groups or classes, distinguished by whether one had advanced a greater or lesser distance along this way. In their Sunday preaching, much thought was given to the "application" to the life of the hearers besides and after the interpretation of the Word. Thus they moved point by point through the differing categories separately. Everyone in the various groups received his or her own word of comfort or admonition.

One great distinction was always made—the distinction between the "converted" ("reborn") and the "unconverted" ("unregenerate"). Ministers proceeded with the notion that among their churchgoers there were, in reality, a number of unconverted. Voetius himself here distinguished among the "lukewarm Christians," the "showy Christians" (who only presented themselves as Christians), and "Sunday Christians" (who obediently sit in church on Sunday, but who know nothing of spiritual inwardness). Others used still other divisions. Sharply admonishing and warning, one turned in particular to the indifferent and to those who wrongly pictured themselves as converted.

A number of divisions were applied to the "converted" as well. That happened mostly with ministers who came later, Bernardus Smytegelt (1665-1739), for instance, a preacher in Zeeland, and Theodorus van der Groe (1705-1784), minister in Kralingen at Rotterdam. They distinguished between the "troubled" and the "refuge-seekers" (those who took their refuge in Christ) and the "assured" (the advanced Christian who had truly found Christ with their hearts). It is to be noted just how those of the first-named category, the "troubled," were thought of. Smytegelt called them, almost fondly, "the crooked reed" (citing Isaiah 42:3), tender and nearly broken plants. He comforted and encouraged them: is not their trouble itself a sign that they are on the good path?

This summary was intended to be more than a description of the different groups of the converted. It was also a typology that everyone could use in one's own spiritual development. Everyone, so Van der Groe maintained, *must* first be "troubled," thus, feel his or her own sinfulness. Only then can and may one flee to Christ. Only so can growth begin and faith deepen and one arrive at a full certainty of faith. Only those who experience what it is to be without God and his salvation can genuinely seek salvation in Christ and can then, ultimately, find him.

Preaching of the Law and Sunday Observance

As already noted, representatives of the Further Reformation placed great emphasis on the necessity of a pure, truly Christian way of life. They sharply rejected loose morality. They advocated great care in the admission to the sacraments. Not every child might simply, without distinction, be baptized regardless of whether the parents were believing Christians. And care had to be taken with the Lord's Supper that "unworthy" persons not partake.

They emphatically set listeners within the purview of God's Law (the Ten Commandments) in their preaching. They gave particular attention to the fourth commandment, concerning the weekly day of rest consecrated to God, the "sabbath." That commandment remains valid, so it was thundered, still unchanged for Christians. What in the Old Testament, in Israel, is the seventh day of the week is for Christians the first day of the week, Sunday.

Participants in the Further Reformation did not want to use the term "Sunday" (originally a pagan term). Rather, critically and ironically, they preferred to speak of "sins-day."[5] That included a sharp condemnation of those who were not very particular about the character of this "day of the Lord."

In any case, this day had to be strictly sanctified. That meant not only participation in church service(s), but also a cessation of work in the hours before and after the services. Thus, strict rest. Even in emergencies (for example, when the harvest threatens to fail due to bad weather and thus must be quickly brought in) there was to be no deviation from the prescribed rest. Sanctification also meant no unnecessary talk, but rather inner attention to the heard proclamation

[5]   *Zonden-dag* ["sins-day"] vs. *zondag* ["Sunday"].

of the Word. This sanctification extended further into the foregoing evening, Saturday evening; one must prepare oneself for the coming day of rest.

Voetians and Cocceians

The struggle for the Further Reformation did not remain uncontested. Others resisted, sometimes in writing, against what in their eyes was an exaggerated emphasis on the Law. Reformation of morals is necessary of course, but, so they argued, it may not be an end in itself. It can only—and that then certainly—come into existence where true belief is preached. One does best to concentrate on *that*.

The critics rejected what they experienced from the representatives of the Further Reformation as exaggerated piety. They saw that expressed in special behavior, special clothing, and in the formation of groups in which some were considered better than others ("so-called Christians").

The interpretation of the Sabbath command became the subject of a fierce controversy that embroiled not only individuals but congregations as well. The critics of the Further Reformation did not want to alter the sanctification of Sunday, but saw the way in which it received its shape not so much as a divine command as an ecclesiastical institution. They saw the principle given in the command to keep one day a week as "sabbath," as a "day of rest," as "moral," and thus remaining valid. But they viewed the concretization given within the command as "ceremonial," i.e., limited in its validity to the Israel of the Old Testament and thus no longer directly applicable for Christians.

Behind this controversy a principled discussion on the interpretation of the Bible as a whole took place. Over and against the vision of Voetius and his colleagues stood that of Johannes Coccejus (1603-1669) and his followers. Coccejus, originally from Germany, was a professor, first at Franeker, and from 1650 at Leiden.

While Voetius proposed a doctrinal system on the basis of the confession and spoke of the Bible in that context, Coccejus, student of the biblical languages, found his thought guided directly by the Bible. He discovered as a red thread running through the entire Bible the story of the covenant that God concludes with humans in order to live "in friendship" with them. With that, he maintained that the making of this covenant is really about a history that took place in a series with various phases. Thus you cannot cite isolated texts from the Bible simply, as divine words, as arguments in an indisputable doctrinal argument. No, each word must be understood in the context of the great Bible story itself. Consideration of faith then is primarily a "thinking-after" from the structure of salvation history witnessed in this story.

Coccejus took special care to distinguish between the phase of the "covenant of works" and that of the "covenant of grace." With the first he alluded to the covenant with Adam, the head of humanity, in paradise. That covenant was based on the presupposition of mutuality: the human is called actually (in his own acts or "works") to love God as God loves him.

As a consequence of human sin, this covenant is broken, "abolished," through the human act. However, God has (so Coccejus read the Bible) held fast to his intention to accompany the human in friendship. He made a covenant with the human anew. The characteristic of this covenant is that it comes from *one* side, as "covenant of grace," and depends on the faithfulness of the *one* Covenant partner, God's own self.

This covenant of grace, however, has not arrived *tout force*. A Mediator was necessary, given by God—his Son, Jesus Christ. The basis must thus lie, so Coccejus maintained, in a pact that, preceding everything, has been made between God the Father and Jesus the Son. With this pact God decided to send Jesus as Mediator and Jesus has made himself available to carry out the work of the Mediator to the salvation of humans.

From his side, the human participates through faith in the covenant of grace, according to Coccejus. The necessity of this belief may not be overlooked. He thus advanced the notion that Jesus' work of mediation does not simply, in itself, mean good for all humans without distinction. In this connection he also spoke of "election." In contrast with the Canons of Dort, however, as well as with Voetius, he rarely used the word. For Coccejus, the full emphasis lay on God's covenant initiative that realizes itself, and continues to realize itself, in the course of time, in the course of salvation history (with the coming of Christ as the decisive moment).

As Voetius had his supporters, so did Coccejus—the "Cocceians." A sharp division arose between the "Voetians" and the "Cocceians," a conflict that continued into the eighteenth century. Among other areas, the conflict came to expression in the manner of preaching in the Sunday service.

The Cocceians gave a less central position to the preaching of the Law of God (the Ten Commandments) than did the Voetians. The Cocceians advocated a freer Sunday observance. They placed more emphasis on objective salvation, given by God in Christ, and less emphasis on the subjective, inward experience of belief of the individual human. Salvation history as proclaimed in the Bible moved them more deeply than the inward development of faith with its various stages that penetrated the human (on the way to or emerging from conversion as the decisive transition).

Their opponents soundly reproached the Cocceians, claiming that they were in fact adherents of the enlightened ideas of Descartes. That reproach was unjust. But it was not completely incomprehensible. The Cocceians were more modern in attitude than the Voetians. They were less stiffly orthodox.

Thus the government found it better to consult with them. In general it was true that the Cocceains circulated in "higher" social circles, while the Voetians found themselves more at the center of the "ordinary folk."

Jean de Labadie and his 'Holy Community'

The strict exercise of discipline (oversight of the way of life of congregational members), as was officially the case in the Reformed Church, had in practice quickly softened. Protests from the Voetians were raised against that state of affairs. One found that there was too little oversight over who participated in the Lord's Supper. Members of the congregation raised objections against having "name Christians" sit together with them at the Lord's Supper. But such protests and objections could still not turn the tide.

The Frenchman, Jean Labadie (1610-1674) preacher of the Walloon congregation (French-speaking) that belonged to the Reformed Church in Middelburg, took his criticism further than the Voetians. He drew the most extreme consequence and viewed the Reformed Church, which in his eyes had become absolutely worldly, no longer as a genuine "church." "Further Reformation" within the context of the church was too little for him; it must be about an absolutely new building.

De Labadie strove for an absolutely holy community, consisting of the purely regenerate. They would have to gather in small circles separately, "conventicles." He quickly came into conflict with the official church. When he continued his activities despite being suspended, he was deposed by the provincial (Walloon) synod. It was the only church division over the course of time that would emerge in the Netherlands until the nineteenth century. De Labadie's supporters, the "Labadists," generally remained a small group.[6]

It happened more often that persons separated themselves privately from the church because they found the church too "broad" or too "lax." They did not always subsequently seek connection with another group. Here and there they formed conventicles[7] where they mutually experienced their brand of piety.

The Eighteenth Century: The Time of the Enlightenment

The eighteenth century was the century of the "Enlightenment"; thus it was a time in which more trust was placed in the human's own capabilities of thought that resulted in correct insight than in the authority of supernatural revelation. Instead of speaking about a "supernatural" or "particular" revelation, one spoke of a "general" revelation that one discovered and knew for oneself through the natural light of reason.

One saw three central religious truths as irrefutably fixed, as everyone could judge: that there is a God, a "Superessence," as the first cause of all that exists; that the human is called to a virtuous life; and that there is an immortal existence in the hereafter in which the human will be rewarded for his virtuous life. One saw in these three truths, evident to reason, the kernel of the Christian faith as well, the summary of what the Bible is really about and what Jesus must have proclaimed.

The remainder of the faith was viewed as less important. In any case, one must no longer debate such matters. In the place of earlier debates and fierce polemic, tolerance would have to emerge. The churches as well would have to write toleration above their doors. They must spend no more thought on their mutual differences; differences do not matter. Above all they must assist humans in becoming virtuous.

For that matter, churches in this time were in fact very respectable bodies. Belonging to church was one element in the lifestyle of the honorable citizen. That was particularly so with the Reformed Church.

---

[6]   A small number of Labadists immigrated to Maryland, where they soon were absorbed into the surrounding population.

[7]   Conventicles were small gatherings of believers where spiritual practices could be exercised and a more experiential form of belief could be shared.

The Church of the 'Fatherland'

Resistance against the spirit of the time still lived in this church. But at the same time it was itself penetrated by the spirit of the time. Life within the church became slack. Little remained of the energy of the early years and the era of the Synod of Dordrecht.

Still, the Reformed Church remained the official, public church in the political system of the Netherlands. Indeed, more and more people spoke of the "Netherlands Reformed Church." The word "reformed" was claimed by the representatives of the Further Reformation particularly for their own endeavor, and thus it received a tone that did not address everyone in the church.

The extent to which the church and the state were seen as one appears from the fact that it was usual for the authorities (the States General) to prescribe days of prayer on the occasion of important events, days on which the entire population was called to prayer for God's blessing and mercy. Ministers of the public church were required to hold church services on the day in question, thereby to preach and to pray.

In the course of the eighteenth century the observance of days of prayer even became a custom that returned each year, apart from special particular events. In that way fixed days of prayer and thanksgiving for crops originated, in March for the first and in November for the latter. Those days were generally observed. Public life came to a halt. No work was done and inns remained closed.

The word "fatherland" began to be used more and more in the eighteenth century as denoting the whole of nation and people. The "fatherland" was thereby seen as something that obligated morality. Citizens were admonished to devote themselves to a virtuous life for the sake of the commonwealth. It was in that context that they were called to prayer by the government. In the government's vision, citizens of the republic were by definition church members, and church members ultimately citizens who loved the fatherland. The Reformed (Netherlands Reformed) Church was not the only church in the Netherlands, but it clearly existed as the "church of the fatherland" par excellence.

CHAPTER 5

The French Period and Beyond: The Church under the Patronage of the State

At the end of the eighteenth century, dissatisfaction and internal tensions were on the increase among the population of the Netherlands. It had been some time since the Republic of the United Netherlands enjoyed the position of power it had attained during the seventeenth ("golden") century. Industry declined. Prosperity decreased. Internal tensions were reinforced by developments elsewhere.

The Batavian Republic

Revolutionary ideas emerged among enlightened writers, primarily in France. They spoke of the "sovereign rights" of the *people* and of the equality of all persons, and their thoughts translated into action. That occurred in the American War of Independence (1775-1783) as well as in the French Revolution. These developments had their impact on the Netherlands.

There had always been a number of opposing positions in the society of the Netherlands. Just so the position of the successive governors (descendants of William of Orange) had been questioned repeatedly. The governors and the States (the regional states and the States-General) were counterparts to each another. At times they were also opponents. The governor (the prince) functioned as advocate for the "common people." The States and the city administrations ("the regents") represented the elite. They retained power to themselves and were reluctant to give it up.

During this time, a new factor came into play: well-to-do, educated citizens. They began to advocate for their own rights. They

49

began to stand over and against the prince and his supporters, "the party of the prince." They called themselves "patriots."

The result was confrontation. The governor (Prince William V) no longer felt safe in Holland. He had lost control over the troops, so he withdrew to the province of Gelderland, where he had greater support. Civil war threatened. In 1787, his brother-in-law, the king of Prussia, came to his help with arms, and the governor was restored to his position of power. Many of his opponents fled to France.

Two years later, the French Revolution took place. At the beginning of 1795, French troops entered the Netherlands. They were welcomed by the "patriots" as liberators. The governor fled to England. That same year the new "Batavian Republic" was proclaimed to take the place of the old Republic. The change would have drastic consequences for the Reformed Church.[1]

Separation of Church and State

On March 1, 1796, the position of the States-General as representative of the populace and as the institution that led the country was taken over in the Batavian Republic by the National Assembly. This was a body chosen by the population through a general suffrage, open to males of the revolutionary party. That body assumed the task of developing a new national administration.

One of the foundational principles of that new administration would be separation of church and state. An end must be made to the privileged position of the Reformed Church. For any particular church to enjoy a similar privilege was to stand in direct contradiction with the principles of the revolution ("freedom, equality, and brotherhood").

Thus on August 5, 1796, the edict was declared: "A privileged or ruling church will no longer be tolerated in the Netherlands."

In addition to the National Assembly, the Provincial States continued to function. For the time being, the regions (provinces) were not inclined to give up their old autonomy. However, when it came to the principle of the separation of church and state, there was no difference of opinion. Already in 1795, prior to the gathering of the National Assembly, the States of the various regions had drawn their own conclusions. It had been decided to make an end of governmental

---

[1] See Simon Schama, *Patriots and Liberators: Revolution in the Netherlands 1780-1813* (New York: Random House, 1977) for a full description of this era in Dutch history.

interference in (Reformed) ecclesiastical matters, as had been the custom since the sixteenth century.

Concretely, the institution of the "political commissioner"—a special representative of the Provincial States to the gatherings of the provincial synods—was curtailed. Henceforth, provincial synods could gather without the presence of representatives of the government, and agreement from the governing authorities would no longer be required.

The involvement of the government in churchly affairs had been brought to an end in yet another matter—the calling of ministers. In a decision of a church council to extend a call to a preacher, consultation with the local government was no longer required.

Ending Reformed Privileges

At the national level, the establishment of a constitution took more time than expected. The constitution became effective May 1, 1798 (following the acceptance by the National Assembly). It included further regulations in the matter of the relation between church and state. The principle of general religious freedom was fundamental. The relevant article reads:

> Each Citizen is free to serve God according to the conviction of his heart. The Society grants in this matter equal freedom and protection to all; provided the public order, established by Law, will never be disturbed by their outward worship.

Of direct significance for the church was the article wherein it was determined that "each Church body is responsible for the maintenance of its Religion, its Ministers and Clergy."

This regulation signaled a formidable problem for the Reformed Church. From the outset it had been accustomed to payment from the government for that maintenance here indicated; that included ministers' salaries. The government had used proceeds from former Roman Catholic possessions that had come under the administration of the state at the end of the sixteenth century for such purposes, and had complemented funds as necessary from its own treasury. This policy would now come to an abrupt end.

It is true that an interim period would be implemented. The salaries of the ministers of the "former Ruling Church" would be paid out of the national treasury for another three years. Thus there would be continued use of ecclesiastical goods, from "spiritual property and funds." However, after three years these goods and funds would be nationalized and used for such purposes as national education and care of the poor. These matters had before been taken care of by the Reformed Church but were now declared to be governmental tasks.

The privileged position of the Reformed Church would be brought to an end in yet another area. It was determined that all Reformed church buildings and manses that were not built by means of the Reformed Church's own funds (that therefore meant all buildings prior to 1580) would be handed over to the local authority, which would subsequently assign them to the largest local church body. Additionally, all other local church bodies would be paid a particular amount on the basis of the assessed value of the buildings thus assigned. The amount of that payment would again depend on the number of members of each of these church bodies. It was supposed that they would, with the help of this payment, be able to care for the subsequent needs of their own local congregations thereafter. Church towers and church clocks would remain the property of the local community.

The Radical Revolutionary Course Adjusted

Understandably, these new regulations evoked much unrest in the Reformed Church. They meant not only an end of privileges, but also an unexpected and enormously increased burden. Would the church, in so short a period as announced, be able to adjust to the new situation?

It did not give in. Provincially and locally, financial commissions were formed. Financial actions were undertaken. Letters of protest were written to the National Assembly as well.

But the political wind soon turned. In France, Napoleon had come to power. He did not intend a (further reaching) radical revolution, so much as he wanted to consolidate what the revolution had already achieved. In the interest of the state, Napoleon tried to establish a positive relationship with the churches. Influenced by this development, a reversal occurred in the Netherlands as well in 1801. The radical revolutionary course of the first years gave way to a more measured policy. In October 1801, the national regulation of 1798 was set aside. A new constitution came into existence. As a matter of course, it maintained the separation of church and state as its starting point. At the outset it set forth the equal privilege of all church bodies. But in fact it was to be considerably more advantageous for the Reformed

Church.

The reassignment of Reformed Church buildings and manses that had earlier been announced did not happen. And the ministers' salaries in the Reformed Church, as the "formerly privileged church," would be paid, at least provisionally, by the government. With an eye to a more definitive regulation, it was determined that the head of each family, as well as each independent person fourteen years and older, must be registered with a church body. Through the state, a yearly tax would be levied for the maintenance of the ministers and the property of one's own church body. Nothing would come of this. But in any case, the state obligated itself, in anticipation and for the future, to stand as guarantor of the financial continuation of the churches—and thus, specifically, the Reformed Church.

An attitude of growing favor toward the churches increased within the government. Religion was considered in the best interest of civil society. Were not all religions, particularly those where "a highest Essence was honored," about the advancement of virtue and good morals? The converse of this new, positive appraisal was of course that the entire business of church bodies again came under the purview of the state. The principle of the separation of church and state apparently did not, in practice, exclude the state from intensive involvement in ecclesiastical life. Governmental participation in the calling of ministers was reinstituted. Henceforth, relevant decisions of the church council would again have to be placed before the local civil administration for approval.

Royal Holland: The French Era

After Napoleon had himself called "caesar" of France in 1804, he desired that areas dependent on France would also realize a central administration, under one head. So in 1806, the Batavian Republic made way for the "Kingdom of Holland," with Napoleon's brother, Louis Napoleon, as king.

In 1806, yet another constitution emerged. In it the king was granted authority to regulate the organization of the church centrally. The new king did not go that far. The "Kingdom of Holland" ended already in 1810, and with it the king's rule. The Netherlands was annexed directly to France.

Still, in the few years the "Kingdom of Holland" existed, Louis Napoleon kept himself intensively busy with ecclesiastical life. In 1807, a number of measures were enacted for economic reasons. In congregations that numbered fewer than two hundred souls, the payment of ministers' salaries from the national treasury was ended. Generally, payments from the national treasury continued to be guaranteed, albeit at the same amount established in 1795. Financial support would continue later, despite the monetary devaluation that would occur. However, as a consequence of the economic crisis, payment in fact did not take place for a rather long time. Poverty was a reality in many manses.

In 1809, for the first time in the history of the Netherlands, an ecclesiastical census was taken. Of the 2.2 million residents of the Netherlands at that time, it appeared that about 55 percent were Reformed.

In the same year, the government established a commission to offer advice in the reorganization of the Reformed Church. A proposed order came into existence that was also recommended to the king. But before it could be adopted, King Louis Napoleon stepped down from the throne and the annexation to France became a fact.

The administration of the Netherlands became more powerfully centralized from Paris. The unified nation-state was introduced, and all traces of the earlier federal system in the "Republic of the United Netherlands" were completely eliminated.

A unified ecclesiastical organization was sought, and that in the national interest. Church divisions that had originated in the previous two centuries must be reversed. Thus, the Reformed and the remonstrants would have to reunite. But the reunification plans stumbled against resistance from the churches. The plans were never executed.

Religion and Church under King William I

The French era came to an end in 1813. In November of that year, the son of the governor who had fled in 1795 (and died in the meantime) returned. Shortly thereafter he was installed as the "Sovereign Prince" in Amsterdam. Irrespective of the French influence, the Netherlands had changed from republic to a monarchy. In 1814, the free Netherlands received its first constitution. Particular advantages gained during the French time were retained. This was so specifically in the equality of all church groups ("religions"). It was expressly decided:

> Equal protection will be given to all existing Religions; their confessors enjoy the same civil privileges and have equal access to

the investiture of positions, offices and ministries.

There still remained a reminder of the earlier, particular connection between the state and the Reformed Church in the prescription:

> The Christian Reformed Religion is that of the sovereign Prince.

But this prescription was scrapped as early as 1815 as a consequence of decisions made in 1814 at the Viennese Congress, when Belgium, overwhelmingly Roman Catholic, had been united with the Netherlands to become one nation. The new nation became a "kingdom" and the prince became King William I.

The financial relationship between church and state continued unchanged. The relevant constitutional article now read:

> The salaries, pensions and all other income, currently being enjoyed by the different religious denominations and their ministers, continue to be assured to the same denominations.

But this financial connection included a new limitation of freedom for the church groups. The king, so it was prescribed, had not only the right of oversight of all denominations, but also and in particular

> The right of inquiry and authority concerning the arrangements of the denominations which...enjoy any payment or arrangements from the National treasury.

Religious matters were considered to be under the king's particular care.

A New *Algemeen Reglement*[2]

This royal concern had to do directly with the Reformed Church. The king deemed a reorganization of this church to be an urgent necessity. The government proposed a new *Algemeen Reglement* for the

---

2   "General Regulations." As will become clear in the text, this document stood at the center of a great deal of controversy in the nineteenth and twentieth centuries. Its promulgation affected the history of the Reformed Church in America, as well as that of the Christian Reformed Church, as it was a major factor in the later separation that further resulted in the nineteenth-century immigration to the United States and the settlements in the Midwest.

administration of the Reformed Church. Thus the proposal that had been drafted already in 1809, during the time of King Louis Napoleon, was brought back into play.

To involve a general synod as representative of the church itself in this proposal for a new church order was a possibility that had been considered in governmental circles. Ultimately, however, that was deemed too cumbersome and superfluous. Instead, the king named eleven ministers as members of a special commission that was to offer advice. This commission was given an opportunity to present its commentary on the proposal that had already been prepared. After the king had amended the proposal in a number of places, it was enacted January 7, 1816, by Royal Decree.

A number of classes protested against the fact that the church order had come into existence without the church having any voice in the matter. However, there was no general protest to speak of. The few protests offered were rejected out of hand. The *"Algemeen Reglement* for the administration of the Reformed Church in the Kingdom of the Netherlands" went into effect April 1, 1816.

One could say that the *Algemeen Reglement* replaced the Dort church order of 1618-1619. That is not entirely correct, however. For as we saw, the Dort church order had never attained the status of a church order that was valid for the entire church. During the era of the Republic of the United Netherlands, the situation differed in each province, both politically and ecclesiastically.

In fact, the *Algemeen Reglement* was the first church order that was applicable for the church in the whole of the Netherlands. Likewise, only with its enactment could it be said straightforwardly that this church, nationally, was organizationally one. Henceforth, the church would officially be called the "Netherlands Reformed Church."

The Administrative Church under the Patronage of the State

It is significant that the church order had as its title: "order for the *administration* of the Reformed Church." Its purpose was exclusively to govern ecclesiastical matters with organizational efficiency. Order must rule in the church, according to 1 Corinthians 14:40: "Let everything be done decently and in good order." This text from the Bible was cited on the seal enacted by the Royal Decree in 1817, that henceforth was to be used by all "higher boards" of the Reformed Church on all acts and letters.

The "higher boards" were the "synod," as "board" of the entire church, and the provincial and classical "boards" over their respective jurisdictions. At the lowest level, in the congregation, the church council was the "board."

Thus, old church names had been retained, but an entirely new, authoritative, administrative system had been introduced using the old names. Remarkably enough, there was no longer any mention of "provincial synods." Certainly "classical gatherings" still existed, but only marginally so. They served almost exclusively to propose lists of candidates to be named to the classical administrations. It was the "boards" that functioned in fact as small directorates in the particular (provincial, classical) jurisdiction—that happened on the national level through the synod, which was nothing more than a synodical "board."

The members of all these boards, including the synod, were named by the king. The first time, that was done directly. Later, members were named from lists of candidates that had been proposed: the appointment of members of the provincial boards on nomination from the classical boards (themselves appointed on nomination by the classical gatherings), the appointment of members of the synod on nomination from the provincial boards. The synod consisted of ten ministers, as representatives not of classes but of the provinces, plus one elder, with a minister (installed in The Hague) as permanent secretary.

'The Synod is not about Doctrinal Differences'

The first gathering of the new synod, in July 1816, was opened with an address from a high government official—the general commissioner of the department of matters concerning the Reformed Church. Speaking in the name of the king, he underscored that the synod need not trouble itself with "theological debates" (differently from its predecessor, the synod of Dort, 1618-1619). For that matter, the synod is, so he said, "not called to decide doctrinal differences, but to administer the church."

He could thereby refer to the article of the *Algemeen Reglement* in which the purpose of the entire ecclesiastical administration was described. According to this article it must be about:

> Care for the interests of Christendom in general as well as the Reformed Church in particular, the maintenance of its doctrine, the multiplication of religious knowledge, the promotion of

Christian morals, the maintenance of order and concord, and the cultivation of love for the King and Fatherland.

It is to be remarked that the "maintenance of doctrine" is named here as one of the tasks of the ecclesiastical administration—and thus of the synod. What that meant, and how this maintenance would take place, is nowhere stated explicitly. When it is claimed that there must be no consideration of adjudicating doctrinal differences, it can only mean the continuance of a doctrinal status quo, by leaving church doctrine undefined and undiscussed.

Later Developments: The Reformed Church Remains an Administrative Church

In 1848 the constitution of the Kingdom of the Netherlands was amended radically. One of the newly accepted principles was the freedom of church bodies to handle their own affairs without interference from the state.

By extension, this amendment of the constitution meant also, in 1852, an amendment of the *Algemeen Reglement*. As was typical of the new situation, this decision was not made by the king, but by the synod. The king subsequently approved the amendment.

The prescription by which the members of ecclesiastical boards were named by the king was eliminated. Ecclesiastical boards at the various levels saw their right to nominate become a right to name members of the various boards.

The order in which the various boards of the Reformed Church occurred was reversed in the new church order: it ran no longer from "above" (the synod) to "beneath" (the church council), but from "beneath" via the mediating levels of classical and provincial boards to "above." For the first time, a prescription was enacted by which it was established that the right to name elders and deacons and to call ministers rested with the congregations. This action was intended to honor the "democratic foundational principle." Thus, one would express the principle that "administration of the church moves up from the congregations to the Synod, which represents the Church."

However, despite all good intentions, the structure of the Reformed Church remained authoritative and administrative. The (small) administrative directorates continued to be decisive on all levels (including the national-synodical).

The article on the purpose of ecclesiastical administration cited above underwent only a few small amendments and additions over the years. The main outlines remained unchanged. That was particularly so of the—still undefined—task of "maintenance of doctrine."

During the nineteenth century the synod was pressed repeatedly for a clear description of what precisely was meant by "the doctrine of the Reformed Church." But the synod refused steadfastly to express itself on the matter. It deemed itself unauthorized. It understood itself primarily called to "administer," that is to say, to the maintenance of order and unity. If the doctrine, the confession, is discussed as to its content, does that not necessarily mean the sowing of dissension?

Dissension would come, however, with greater frequency, clearly and fiercely. The nineteenth century would come to represent the sharp opposition of schools of thought.

CHAPTER 6

Emerging Conflict:
Moderns and Orthodox

In the nineteenth century a number of fierce conflicts broke out within the Netherlands Reformed Church, conflicts that would continue into the twentieth century. We saw that the "synod," established by the king in 1816 as a new national administrative organ of the church, deemed itself neither authorized nor called to express itself in doctrinal questions. The supposition was that by refusing to opt for one or another party on matters that involved the substance of questions of faith, the synod acted in the interest of the church. In this way, it was thought, the unity of the church could be maintained. That, however, appeared to be an illusion.

Conflict over the Proponents' Formula

All too quickly, conflict flared on the question of how the proponents' formula (also established in 1816) was to be interpreted.[1] This formula included the declaration that future ministers must sign before they were allowed to become preachers.

The formula in effect prior to 1816 (by virtue of the decision of the synod of Dort, 1618-1619), stated that the articles of faith contained in the three classic Reformed confessional writings (the "formulae of unity") "agreed in everything with God's Word." Future

---

[1] See Gerrit J. ten Zythoff, *Sources of Secession: The Netherlands Hervormde Kerk on the Eve of the Dutch Immigration to the Midwest* (Grand Rapids: Eerdmans, 1987), 43 f.

ministers had to promise by their signature that they "will diligently teach and faithfully advocate" this doctrine.

However, in 1816, a new proponents' formula was established by the newly seated synod. According to this formula, future ministers must promise to profess that "the doctrine which, in agreement with God's Holy Word, is contained in the accepted formulae of unity of the Netherlands Reformed Church."

Is that not substantially the same? Not exactly. In any case, it is ambiguous. What does "in agreement with God's Holy Word" mean? Is it *because* or *insofar as* it (the doctrine) agrees with God's Word? In the latter case the formula allows space for some distance from the particular views of the confessional writings.

This last interpretive possibility was rejected out of hand in a number of polemical publications. Some critics were of the opinion that the new proponents' formula in fact "slyly and subtly" undermined orthodox doctrine. The synod was now urged to express itself on this formal question at least.

That took place in 1841. The synod maintained that not *everything* in the confessional writings must be viewed as agreeing with God's Word *per se*. It also underscored that in the required declaration it was not about agreement with this or that literal truth of the confessional writings, but—more globally—about agreement with the "doctrine" that was determined there "in essence and in the main."

Those who were oriented as moderns[2] could live very well with this formulation. In their understanding, there was sufficient room in the church. The orthodox, faithful to the confessions, felt themselves less at home. They strove to have the church (the synod) actively maintain the official confession, including the admittance of students to the pulpit.

In 1888, the synod again made it clear that it wanted neither to amend nor to interpret the proponents' formula in a more orthodox sense. A new formula was yet again enacted. Henceforth signatories would be asked to promise

> to proclaim the Gospel of Jesus Christ in agreement with the principles and the character of the Reformed Church in this nation and to promote the interests of the kingdom of God and those of the Netherlands Reformed Church according to one's

---

[2]   "Modern" describes a way of understanding the faith that will be described later in the text under "modernism."

ability.

It is remarkable that the confessional writings are no longer mentioned here. What is meant by "the Gospel of Jesus Christ" remains undetermined. In later years, repeated proposals for amendment were submitted. Some wanted to see a reference to the confessional writings included again. But such proposals were rejected by the synod piece by piece. The proponents' formula established in 1888 remained unchanged until 1951, the year that an entirely new church order was introduced.

Groningen Theology

In the meantime, the synod could count on the agreement of many in its refusal to accede to the maintenance of the confessional writings. About the year 1830, a new theology emerged under the leadership of a number of professors at Groningen (among whom Petrus Hofstede de Groot, 1802-1886, was the most prominent). This new theology did not intend to detract from the authority of the Bible, but principally set itself against any sort of imposition of doctrine. One spoke of "Groningen theology." It quickly became popular.

In contrast with the (Calvinist) doctrine, advocates of Gronigen theology put Jesus, and passionate surrender to him as the living Lord, at the center. This surrender in faith in their view meant above all that one allows oneself to be inspired by, "educated in," Jesus' example to a life of love and toleration. Thereby one could, they claimed, also become more and more victorious over human sin. The church, as an "educational institution," exists to stimulate this process.

This theology agreed perfectly with the synodical policy and with the vision of ecclesiastical administration that had been articulated in the *Algemeen Reglement*. That document speaks of such matters as the "multiplication of religious knowledge," "promotion of Christian morals," "maintenance of order and unity," and "cultivation of love for King and Fatherland." In that context, the words "maintenance" of "doctrine" are out of place. Above all, the church is to be a useful institution for the society (promoting concord, loving the Fatherland, royalist). As it would later be stated in the proponents' formula of 1888, the church's ministers must be those who tend to "the interests of the kingdom of God." Certainly. But that "kingdom of God" could not in turn (thus according to a comment at the time) be much different from that of an ideal Society for Public Welfare.

This theology has been called "crises-less" or "just kind-hearted." The notion that a radical break (in "sin") opened up between God and the human was strange to it. Thus, its supporters distanced themselves from orthodox Calvinism as expressed by the seventeenth-century Synod of Dort. They also could not begin with the thought (defended in the Canons of Dort) of an eternal divine decision to the "election" of some and the "rejection" of others.

"Groningen theology" continued into the 1860s as popular and influential within the Reformed Church.

The *Afscheiding*[3]

There were, however, counter voices. They came mainly from two sides: from the circles of the *Reveil* and from supporters of the *Afscheiding* (in 1834).

This last named movement was the result of deep dissatisfaction over ecclesiastical synodical policy. That dissatisfaction existed primarily in the northern provinces. It gained a public voice in the emergence and the publications of Hendrik de Cock (1801-1842), minister from 1829 in Ulrum in the province Groningen (where he was the successor to Hofstede de Groot).

Gradually, De Cock came under the influence of Calvinist orthodoxy, in particular of the classic Reformed doctrine of election. He displayed this interest in his preaching. People came from a great distance to his church. At the request of some of these supporters who came from elsewhere, he baptized their children. That was frowned on by his colleagues, the neighboring ministers. A number of them wrote publicly about De Cock's ideas and viewed his actions critically. De Cock reacted with the publication of a fierce pamphlet. Thus the criticism of his activities continued to grow.

The board of the classis felt itself forced to make an example of De Cock. In December 1833—just before Christmas—De Cock was suspended from preaching, not on account of the content of his preaching (the administrative church neither could nor would speak to matters of faith) but for formal reasons. He was condemned as a disturber of the peace, for his "insulting" and "loveless" activities.

---

3   Or "separation." As noted in the introduction, this movement was to be of fundamental importance to American Reformed bodies of Dutch extraction, as it was to provide the occasion for the nineteenth-century Dutch immigration to the United States.

De Cock did not intend schism. For the time being, he subjected himself to ecclesiastical censure. He appealed, of course, to the provincial ecclesiastical board, and further, to the synod. In July 1834, he was deposed by the synod, if he would not show himself repentant and obedient within half a year.

Sympathizers encouraged him to continue on the new path. In October 1834, it indeed came to a break. De Cock drafted an *Act of Separation ("Afscheiding") or Return*, which was signed by his church council and the great majority of his congregation. In this *Act* it was stated that the Netherlands Reformed Church was viewed as a "false church," and there was to be no more "communion" with this church "until it returned to the truthful service of the Lord." It was also declared, to the contrary, that communion "with all true Reformed members" was desired and that in everything one wanted to adhere to the "old formulae of unity." It was stated, finally, that De Cock was recognized as "our legitimately called and ordained Pastor and Teacher." Other congregations, and groups from other congregations, quickly aligned themselves with the Ulrum initiative.

The *Afscheiding* almost immediately provoked reaction from the Reformed Church (the synod) as well as from the government. In October 1834, the general synodical commission (that had functioned as the executive committee of the synod since 1827) requested, by letter, that the government intervene, which it did promptly. The activities of De Cock and his supporters were seen as disturbing the order of society. The authorities themselves wanted to suppress any threat to order and rest. That was particularly the case because shortly before this time (in 1830) the Belgic uprising had occurred, and the Belgic regions had become a nation separate from the Netherlands. Police and the military took action against the separatists. Their church services were forbidden and scattered. Their families were required to quarter soldiers. Leaders (including De Cock himself) landed in prison.

Had there not been a constitutional equality of all church groups in the Netherlands since 1814? Yes, and the separatists appealed expressly to that provision. But their appeal was in vain. The government pointed out that no separated church group had existed in 1814, and that thus the separatists could not claim constitutional protection.

The separatists persisted, however. Their support was not great (according to official numbers in 1836, it was only a few thousand), but they were determined and prepared to sacrifice. The repression under which they lived gradually eased. They formed their own congregations. As a consequence of the constitutional change of 1848, freedom of religion and its practice was declared to apply to them as well.

It was a while before they could present themselves nationally as one church body. That became the case in 1869. The church group accepted the name "Christian Reformed [*Gereformeerde*] Church." The word *gereformeerde* took up again the old name of the Reformed Church; they understood themselves to be the true continuance of the past. Thus far, "reformed" [*hervormde*] and *gereformeerde* had been two names of the same church. For the first time, *gereformeerde* was given the specific meaning of self-distinction from the Netherlands Reformed Church through the express acceptance of the classic Reformed confessional documents (and of the Dort church order) of the Reformed Church.

The *Reveil* [4]

The *Afscheiding* was supported primarily by small business folk, workers, day laborers, and small farmers in the northern provinces. In contrast, the *Reveil* found its support primarily among aristocratic circles in Amsterdam and The Hague. Class difference was in part the reason that, while folk from the *Reveil* certainly sympathized with the *Afscheiding*, they did not join it.

The *Reveil* was a revival movement. Similar revival movements were occurring contemporaneously in England, Switzerland, and France. One of the first expressions of the movement in the Netherlands was the 1823 publication of the pamphlet *Bezwaren tegen den geest der eeuw* [E.T. *Objections to the Spirit of the Age*] by Isaac da Costa (1798-1860), who had converted recently from Judaism to Christianity. The pamphlet was a fierce protest against the lax, unprincipled spirit of the age (regnant both within and outside the church), against everything that could be called "modern." It was also a passionate call to true faith and to an acknowledgment of God's sovereignty over life.

Participants in the *Reveil* desired primarily a conversion of the heart. They dedicated themselves to biblical studies and held religious practices in homes. Thus the *Reveil* was, in a sense, a continuation of the seventeenth and eighteenth century "Further Reformation." Supporters of the *Reveil* found support for their efforts in the Reformed confessional writings. Thus, they also zealously advocated the recovery

---

4   Or "revival." Although this will be described as a European movement of awakening of faith, it needs to be distinguished from American revivals that would take on different characteristics.

of the authority of those documents, an authority that, in their opinion, had rightly been granted to them in the church of the past.

It was no wonder that they sympathized with the *Afscheiding*. However, they did not want to break with the Reformed Church. The struggle for truth must be advanced not outside but within the church—so they maintained.

Under the leading of the historian and lawyer, Guillaume Groen van Prinsterer (1801-1876), the battle was powerfully taken in hand. At the same time, petitions were pressed on the synod for it to do what was officially part of its set of responsibilities: formally and juridically to maintain doctrine, including the practice of discipline. Not only ministers, but members of the Reformed Church as well, would have to subscribe to the confessional documents, or else draw the consequences and leave the church.

Hermann Friedrich Kohlbrugge

Hermann Friedrich Kohlbrugge (1803-1875) played a special role in all these events. On the one hand, he shared the dissatisfaction of the *Reveil* over the lukewarmness in the church. His critical attitude even meant that he would not be admitted as a minister in the Reformed Church.

On the other hand, he could not agree with the emphasis in the circles of the *Reveil* that was laid on the necessity of personal conversion and sanctification of life. In his preaching, he emphatically argued that Christ had come to stand perfectly in the place of the human, and thus the human *is* already wholly "justified" and "holy." To the question of when a human had been converted, he answered, "In Christ's cross and resurrection."

A similar emphasis on the objective nature of salvation in Christ was completely strange to the people of the *Reveil*. A powerful conflict emerged between Kohlbrugge and De Costa. Ultimately, Kohlbrugge went his own, lonely way. That was true not only theologically; he became the leader of a group of Reformed congregational members in the German village of Elberfeld. Later, we shall see how his thoughts would again take effect in the twentieth century and would initiate a complete renewal of theology and the church.

Modernism

At the same time, on the other end of the spectrum a radical movement took over from the Groningen theology. It was "modernism."

Its primary representatives were Cornelis Willem Opzoomer (1821-1892, professor at Utrecht) and Jan Hendrik Scholten (1811-1885, professor at Leiden).

Groningen theology had, with all its new ideas, continued to cling tightly to the notion that God is a peculiar, supernatural Reality who intervenes in our world from above. That thought (including the notion of the possibility of miracles as encroachment on natural laws) was completely dismissed under the influence that new scientific inquiry made on Opzoomer and Scholten. Certainly, they continued to talk about the "divine," but by that they meant that the divine revealed itself *in* the human, in his particular thinking, willing and feeling, and was not directed *to* the human from without. "God" does not stand over and against nature, but is the center of all reality—that is itself the revelation of God.

The Bible was certainly valued by the moderns, but it was not seen as the peculiar, normative, divine authority before which the human must prostrate himself in faith. The Bible functioned as a human book, the expression of human faith. Christians could still, in the present, recognize their own faith in the Bible. But God's Word— spoken of as the "voice of the Holy Spirit"—speaks no less within human reason than in the Bible.

It was also the moderns who found themselves inspired by the new, critical, biblical inquiry already practiced for some time in Germany; furthermore, they participated in it. Upon closer view, there appeared to be a number of repetitions, improbabilities, and absurdities in the Bible. That appeared to provide more than sufficient reason to doubt the historical reliability of the gospels. The gospels were seen more as utterances of primitive folk belief, or as literary expressions of religious feelings. Even at their best, they are human writings.

The Old Testament was also investigated in a comparable manner. Pathbreaking work was done by Abraham Kuenen (1828-1891, professor at Leiden). He concluded that the first five "books of Moses" had in reality originated centuries after Moses' era, and that they were the result of a complex process of the confluence of pieces from various sources.

Belief must now be completely thought out anew. That was done foundationally by Scholten. In 1848, he published his *De leer der Hervormde Kerk*[5], a book that was to undergo further revisions

---

5   "The Doctrine of the Reformed Church."

and a variety of reprintings. The aim of this book was not to describe the various dogmas and doctrines as they stood in the confessional documents. As he saw it, traditional doctrines were untenable, to say nothing of the impossibility that they be imposed as required as truths of faith (after the manner of the Synod of Dort, 1618-1619). Instead, Scholten wanted to identify the "principles" that had always provided the foundation of official doctrine and that remain valid for the modern person because they were acceptable to reason. He specifically viewed one such as "the acknowledgment of God's absolute overlordship."

To Scholten's conviction, anyone who observes the creation can conclude that there must be a First Cause of everything—God. The human who recognizes this accepts God all the more as the all-determining power of his willing and acting. The one who has done so absolutely and in an exemplary way is Christ. Thus in him, God's activity-in-the-world becomes palpable. The slumbering divine construction that is in every human came to complete expression in Christ. Now the same can happen in the life of everyone who follows Christ. Thus the human becomes the servant of God; inspired by Christ's example, he himself understands, autonomously, God's Word in his own spirit. That is what matters in Christendom; it would remain true even if Christ had not lived historically. Christian belief does not depend on the person of Christ, but on the doctrine Jesus brought, or at least that was ascribed to him.

Such ideas, proposed in a university setting, also found their way to the congregation. The results of the new, critical biblical inquiry became well known in a wide circle. Particular incidents attracted much attention. For example, on Easter Sunday, 1866, three preachers, by mutual arrangement, stated from the pulpit that they could no longer believe in the bodily resurrection of Christ. They were not the only ones who expressed themselves this way. Take the utterance of another who, at a celebration of the Lord's Supper, said that the supper means nothing other than "the memory of the death of a friend whom we esteemed and loved." Or the fact that at baptism a number of ministers changed the classic formula, "I baptize you in the name of the Father and of the Son and of the Holy Spirit," to baptism "to belief, hope and love" or "to the initiation into Christendom," or simply did away with any special formula.

Some moderns could no longer reconcile their ideas with their membership in the church. They left, although most continued to call themselves Christians. Opzoomer also distanced himself from the Reformed Church. In 1870, he became one of the founders of the "Netherlands Protestant Covenant," a union that had as its goal the promotion of the "free development of the religious life...both within the circles of Church groups and without." The Protestant Covenant decisively did not and does not desire to be a "church." One need not give up one's church membership to become a member. Nonetheless, the Protestant Covenant was seen by some as the new, liberal church by means of which all other churches would eventually become superfluous.

Most supporters of the modern party,[6] however, did not want to break with the church. They preferred to bring the church "up to date" and thereby to give it new opportunities for the future (it was not for nothing that Scholten titled his book, "The doctrine of the Reformed Church"). They stayed at their posts, firmly refusing to be deprived of their right to a place within the Reformed Church.

Battle at the Ballot Box: The Confessional Union

That right, however, was definitely not undisputed. Modernist notions caused a great commotion, primarily among orthodox church members. Petitions continued to pour in at the annual gathering of the synod with requests to intervene and actively to maintain the classic Reformed confessional documents.

The requests did not have a positive result; the synod continued to react negatively and adopted a neutral attitude. However, other actions from the orthodox side did succeed. That happened particularly in the calling of orthodox ministers and the naming of orthodox elders and deacons.

As a consequence of the new political ideas (the new constitution of 1848, a new vision of the relation between church and state), the *Algemeen Reglement* of the Reformed Church was changed (as we saw in the previous chapter) in 1852 (and with royal approval). One of the

6   *Richting.* Literally, the term means "direction." The Dutch themselves would later use the term, "modality." It came to have a very important meaning in Dutch church life in the nineteenth and twentieth century. It described various theological schools of thought. Increased *richtingen strijd*, or party strife, would characterize the Dutch theological world. It would also provide the occasion for the renewal of the Netherlands Reformed Church in the 1940s and 1950s. The classic work is Th. L. Haitjema, *De Richtingen in De Nederlandse Hervormde Kerk* (Wageningen: Veenman & Zonen, 1934).

changes concerned the naming of elders and deacons and the calling of preachers. The naming and the calling would henceforth be granted as a right of the congregation itself.

It would certainly be a while before this right was actively regulated and introduced. In 1867, the relevant system for choice became active. Among other matters, it was determined that in large congregations the right of choice was practiced by an electoral college in which, beside the members of the church council, a double number, chosen by the congregation, would have a seat.

As a consequence of this and similar regulations a genuine electoral war broke out in many places. In many congregations where the church council was of the modern party, the orthodox party was successful in putting its own representatives in the electoral college and in the church council, even winning the majority. Clearly, the result was that a number of places that previously had modern ministers began to call orthodox ministers.

The synod viewed this turn of events with alarm. It regretted the mutual embitterment and intolerance in the church, but it saw no way to end it.

The orthodox had also organized themselves nationally. Already in 1864, partly on the initiative of Groen van Prinsterer (of the *Reveil*), a group had been established that after 1865 would be called the "Confessional Union." The starting point of this union was "an open and unambiguous agreement with the foundation of the church, contained in its confessional writings." It was zealous that the confession would be honored everywhere in the church as the real "condition of ecclesiastical communion." It was intended to counter what they viewed as further "degradation" of the church and to contribute to the restoration of the church. To that end they saw it as their task to establish particular gospel stations in Reformed congregations that had suffered under modernist ministers and to bring to an end the actual doctrinal freedom in the church. With this last objective in mind, the church order (the *Algemene Reglement*) would have to be changed—by "legal means" of course. Thus the union stood militantly opposed to the policy of the synod.

"Confessionals" (as they would henceforth be called) and moderns (or "liberals") came to stand directly over and against one another. The confessionals demanded, as had the *Reveil* earlier, juridical maintenance of the confession, and that included the practice of discipline of doctrine. The liberals demanded freedom in doctrine.

These standpoints remained deeply rooted. There could be no talk of meeting.

The *Doleantie*[7]

Further oppositions within the church were aggravated by the emergence of Abraham Kuyper (1837-1920). As minister at Utrecht (1867-1870) and at Amsterdam (from 1870), he developed a conscious strategy by which the orthodox would be able to effect a true "reformation" of the church. It would be a reformation that, he argued (and thereby went a step further than the confessionals), must break if necessary with the existing ecclesiastical organization, or at least with the existing "ecclesiastical bond."

The starting point was his notion that a principal difference exists between Christians and non-Christians, a difference that must have its impact on society. True Christians devote themselves to effecting the "Spirit of Christ" in all areas of life. To that end they should organize in their own societal context. Thus Kuyper became a fierce advocate of the principle of pillarization.[8] He left no doubt that it was his conviction that (Reformed) Protestantism was to the purest form of Christendom.

In connection with the above, it was his conviction that the church as well must clearly be determined by this "Spirit of Christ." The church, so Kuyper argued, is essentially the gathering of genuine believers, the communion of those confessing. A church (organization) that does not take the right of confession seriously (because it does not really maintain it) cannot claim the name "church." An ecclesiastical administration that no longer stands for the truth has no right of acknowledgment from those who know themselves assuredly obligated to the truth, as laid down in the confession. The latter must then claim their freedom in the matter of principled questions and go their own way as a congregation as local "church." They need no longer be subject to ecclesiastical regulations of an "unreformed" ecclesiastical administration.

These notions found a great echo in the Reformed congregation

---

[7]   The "Sorrowing" or "Complaining."

[8]   Pillarization (*verzuiling* in Dutch) describes a unique Dutch arrangement by which various sectors of society were compartmentalized into separate "pillars." Each group, e.g., Roman Catholics, would have its own schools, labor unions, newspapers, political parties, radio networks, etc.

in Amsterdam, particularly in the church council. Public protest by orthodox elders emerged there against the work of some liberal ministers. The split spread beyond Amsterdam. In April 1883, representatives of congenial church councils gathered in Amsterdam. The gathering concluded that the "church bond of 1816" must be broken where it hindered the "honoring of Jesus as King in his church." It was also decided that those who were faithful to the confessions in congregations under the leadership of a liberal church council would have to break with that church council and must *dolerend* (regretfully, i.e., under protest) establish their own church in that locality.

Events were set intentionally on a collision course with higher ecclesiastical administrations. The conflict occurred in 1884, when the church council of Amsterdam refused to admit to public confession of faith a number of students (candidates for confirmation) taught by liberal ministers. That refusal was in part a protest against the vaguely formulated confessional questions in effect at that time in the Reformed Church by virtue of synodical policy. When the candidates requested an attestation of their good moral conduct in order that they might be accepted as confessing members in another congregation, the church council demanded of the petitioners an additional, special confession (as the orthodox understood it) as a condition. The candidates rejected this condition as arbitrary and unjustified. Consequently, the church council decided not to accede to their request.

The candidates introduced a complaint against this decision of the church council with the classical board, and later with the provincial ecclesiastical board as well. The complainants were judged in the right. The church council appealed to the synod. It received the reaction it had expected (and desired); the synod confirmed the decision and ordered the church council to grant the attestations within six weeks—that meant before January 8, 1886. To the church council of Amsterdam, placed in the wrong as a result of their "faithfulness to the confession," the ecclesiastical organization clearly revealed itself as "unfaithful" and "spiritually powerless."

In view of the unavoidable break with the "church bond," the church council quickly introduced an amendment to the regulations that guided the financial administration of the church in Amsterdam in December 1885. The change was meant to guarantee that the property of the Amsterdam congregation (buildings, manses) would remain under the control of the church council, even if it was suspended or deposed.

Deposition did in fact take place, precisely on the basis of this decision concerning the financial administration. On January 4, 1886, the eighty members of the church council who had supported the decision were from that date suspended from performance of their office by the classical board in an emergency meeting. Thus a formal church council in Amsterdam no longer existed. The classical board took over the tasks of the church council (according to the regulations). It was also free to act in the matter that had been the occasion of the conflict: the requested attestations were granted to the catechetical candidates. On July 1, 1886, the suspension was changed by the provincial ecclesiastical administration to deposition from office. This judgment affected seventy-five of the eighty members of the church council (the remaining five had, after further thought, announced that they had changed their thinking).

This decision was also appealed to the synod by those affected. On December 1, 1886, this appeal was rejected; the deposition of the seventy-five members of the church council was a fact.

On December 16, the deposed members held a gathering in which they called themselves the "reappeared legitimate church council of Amsterdam." News of this action was given by special report to both the members of the congregation and to the governing authorities. It was stated that an end had been made, without delay, "to the deadly embrace by which the Synodical Hierarchy threatened to squeeze the life out of the Reformed Church of Amsterdam" and that one had "thrown off" the "yoke" of this "Synodical Hierarchy." It was expressly declared *not* to have separated from the old church of the Reformation, but precisely through its act of throwing off the "synodical yoke" to *remain* in the church. Members of the congregation were called to follow the members of the church council in their break with the "Synodical Hierarchy." About twenty-five thousand congregational members did so.

However, not all the Reformed in Amsterdam took this step. The movement resulted in a congregational split. It spread beyond Amsterdam. Elsewhere, entire congregations along with their pastors walked out of the "Reformed Church Bond." In the beginning of 1886, that had already happened in Kootwijk and Voorthuizen. In most cases a split occurred, just as it had in Amsterdam. This division often went through entire families, even homes, and led to a good deal of mutual bitterness and estrangement. Those who left subsequently formed a particular local *"gereformeerde* church" alongside the continuing

Reformed congregation.

In January 1887, representatives from the church councils of all the congregations that had left the synodical church gathered in Amsterdam for a four-day congress. Kuyper was the central speaker and guiding spirit. The gathering of participants was overwhelmingly large. There was consultation on the question of how others, congregations and ecclesiastical institutions, could be induced to throw off the "synodical yoke." Models of action were proposed; advice was offered.

It was decided that congregations that had left the Reformed Church would be called *dolerend*, following the example of Amsterdam. It was thus claimed that one complied only under protest with a situation in which the Reformed church property (churches and manses) remained under the control of Reformed congregations that been left behind. The name, *Doleantie*, was used as an indication of this entire movement of exodus from the Reformed Church bond as it had originated under Kuyper's inspiration.

The *dolerenden* (regretful separatists) quickly formed their own national church bond. Their synod was formed of representatives from the congregations. In 1892, both separation movements united in what since is called the *Gereformeerde Kerken* (Reformed Churches) *in the Netherlands*. Not all the descendants of the 1834 separation movement could find themselves in this church union. A minority continued in the "Christian Reformed Church." In 1947, this church body amended its name to the plural, "Christian Reformed Churches." Both church bodies intended (at least in principle) to return to the Dort Church Order in the regulation of their peculiar organizations.

CHAPTER 7

After the *Doleantie*:
Struggle for Church Renewal

The *Doleantie* resulted in heavy bloodletting for the Netherlands Reformed Church. All in all, seventy-six of its ministers and more than two hundred church councils subscribed to the *Doleantie*, along with about nine percent of its members. The coreligionists were overwhelmingly lower class. Besides being a faith movement, the *Doleantie* was an emancipation movement. Kuyper knew how to mobilize his followers in societal matters as well.

According to the census of 1889, it appeared that of a total of about 4.5 million residents, the percentage of Reformed, compared with 1879, had declined from 54.5 to 48.88 percent; the percentage of *gereformeerden* had risen in the same ten years from 3.5 (when it included only the *afgescheidenen*) to 8.21 percent (the *afgescheidenen* and the *dolerenden* together).

Philippus Jacobus Hoedemaker

Kuyper had expected greater success from the *Doleantie*. It grieved him particularly that not all the orthodox within the Reformed Church had chosen his party. The orthodox who had remained in the Reformed Church shared the concern for orthodox confession that Kuyper and his supporters had initiated, but they did not want to break from the church.

Their prominent spokesman (and thus the direct opponent of Kuyper) was Philippus Jacobus Hoedemaker (1839-1910). He was originally a supporter of Kuyper. As a minister in Amsterdam, he had even been drawn into Kuyper's plans to establish a new university (on a Reformed foundation). The Free University was, in fact, established in Amsterdam in 1880. Hoedemaker accepted a professorship in it. However, in the end he distanced himself from Kuyper on account of Kuyper's partisanship. In 1887, he resigned his professorship and again became a minister in the Netherlands Reformed Church.[1]

His aim is summarized in the title of one of his writings: *Heel de Kerk en heel het volk*.[2] For him it was a matter of holding firmly to the confession *within* the whole of the Reformed Church. That whole was dear to him. He viewed the action of leaving the church because it was unfaithful to its confession and because of its unfortunate organizational structure (since 1816) as an easy out, in essence as sectarian.

To his way of thinking, the path of party struggle should not be chosen within the church. When those faithful to the confessions would have won the majority in various boards, they would still have won nothing. Above all else, one must learn that the church is something different from a union or a society. A union is always established by humans. A person can make himself a member of a union by virtue of his own decision; one can also resign from membership. It is different in the church. It is brought together by its Lord, Jesus Christ. It rests on the foundation of God's covenant. Humans belong to the church not by virtue of their own decisions, but by virtue of the covenant that God made with humans and that proceeds from parents to children (hence infant baptism as well). The human is a member of the church not by choice, but by birth.

Even so, Hoedemaker deemed that a reorganization of the Reformed Church was urgently necessary. The administrative organization of 1816 would indeed have to be abolished. No administration, neither higher nor lower, could do service in the church. Christ calls humans to office in the midst of the congregation. In its office-bearers, the church itself is represented. Whether they gather locally (as church council), classically, provincially, or even nationally,

---

[1] American readers might be interested to know that Hoedemaker spent several years in the United States. He attended New Brunswick Theological Seminary for a year, completed seminary at a Congregational institution in Chicago, and served several congregations in southern Michigan. He also became active in Democratic politics, participating in the presidential campaign of James Buchanan.

[2] "The whole church and the whole people."

makes no difference to the authority of the gathering. It is precisely in a church so organized that the confession can live, so said Hoedemaker. To desire to maintain the confession juridically (and in the Reformed Church with its present organization it would not be possible to do so in any other way) as a petrified document makes no sense.

In Hoedemaker's thought, God's covenant stands at center. He believed this covenant to be relevant not only for the church, but for the entire (Dutch) people. He emphatically viewed the Netherlands as a Protestant-Christian nation. While Kuyper resigned himself to the reality that matured in the nineteenth century, the neutral state, Hoedemaker pled for a Christian state, or at least for a "State with the Bible." To know its task, the government would have to open itself to the judgment and the biblical interpretation of the church.

In Hoedemaker's conception, the church may not withdraw into a ghetto or into antitheses. It must become a *volkskerk*. He did not mean by that a church to which all residents of the nation, all the citizens of the state, would, by definition, belong. He meant a church that is in missionary service to the entire people, a confessing church in the midst of the life of the *volk*.

With such notions, Hoedemaker appeared to revert in part to the pre-1795 situation of the Republic of the United Netherlands. However, what he had in mind had not in fact been a reality at that earlier time, neither in the state nor in the church.

Hoedemaker found adherence to his struggle, his ideal of a *volkskerk*, in the Confessional Union. He became a member and for a time was its president. In 1888, he began the publication of the weekly newspaper *De Gereformeerde Kerk*, which is still the organ of the Confessional Union, although under a different name, *Confessioneel*, and now as a fortnightly paper. In 1893, this union accepted new by-laws. Among other things, they stated:

> That the Reformed Church of this nation, existing under abnormal conditions long before 1816, is nonetheless a true Church of Christ and on the basis of its confession and irrevocable rights must be seen as the only legitimate continuation of the Church, as it manifested itself in the days of the Reformation, purified of errors.

And in conclusion:

> That thereby the vocation of the believer is to remain in the Church and not...to break the church bond; indeed to work

within the church and for its restoration.

Hoedemaker's ideas can be recognized in these formulations.

Still, Hoedemaker's relationship with the Confessional Union would not be of long duration. In 1897, he resigned as a member out of fear that partisanship would present itself there as well. He has been typified appropriately as an "incomprehensible thinker." That phrase expresses something of the lonely path he trod. However, his ideas would later make their way. They would become of enormous significance in the renewal of the Netherlands Reformed Church in the twentieth century.

'Ethical' Theology

In the midst of the opposition between the modernists and the confessionals, one group in the Reformed Church could find itself in neither camp. Inspired by the *Reveil*, these Christians had developed the notion that truth is "ethical." By that they meant that truth does not only concern thinking (which makes confessional formulas matters of debate) but is also and primarily a matter of the heart, touching life. The word "ethical" is derived from "ethos," i.e., inner existence, disposition.

The pioneers in this strain of thought were Daniel Chantepie de la Saussaye (1818-1874) and Johannes Hermanus Gunning (1829-1905). Both had been ministers for a number of years and in later life were called to the professorship (the first in Groningen and the latter in Amsterdam and Leiden).

Faith, so they maintained, is first of all a matter of a living, existential meeting with God. It is to have a relationship with Christ. God has not revealed God's self through dogmatic teaching or through a series of truths of faith, but rather in communicating God's self to the human. That means renewal of life for the human.

The church is primarily a communion of humans inspired by this new life in community with Christ. That it has an outward, organizational, form is secondary. It may never be identified with an unchangeable administrative apparatus. Belief comes to expression in a confession, but it is never captured by confession. Confession is above all a living, moving matter, always emerging anew from the hearts of humans, in answer to the contemporary problems that are set before them.

Thus it is disastrous to want to impose a fixed confession as binding. Unity of faith within the church cannot be juridically enforced.

Such would stand in direct conflict with the understanding that the truth with which faith has to do is rooted in living reality, "life." This truth must itself be allowed to exercise its effect in the human heart. Juridical disciplinary measures are only hindrances here, with however good intentions they may be defended. One should not expect them from the synod either. The practice of discipline must be of a medical nature—the stimulation of healing powers. It must be intended not to cut the sick off but to save them.

Of course, these ideas found remarkably little sympathy with the confessionals. They saw them as too vague, not sufficiently concrete. Still a rapprochement arose between Gunning and Hoedemaker. Gunning joined Hoedemaker in his struggle for a reorganization of the church. Together with Hoedemaker, he sent an open letter to the synod (without any effect) in 1904 with concrete proposals for reorganization. He was more and more convinced that the way the church is organized was not to be seen spiritually as an unimportant matter.

In contrast to the confessionals, the "ethicals" had not yet formed their own organization. Their influence in the church was primarily indirect. It was in 1921 that the Ethical Union was established.

The *Gereformeerde Bond*[3]

Some of the confessionals were not happy with the policy of their own union and wanted a more aggressive stance. In particular they could not find themselves in the ideal of the people's church that Hoedemaker had introduced. Was not such a broad goal for the church to be won at the cost of the loss of acknowledgment of the authority of the full confession? What, for example, remains of the doctrine of election confessed in the Canons of Dort?

The *Gereformeerde Bond* was established on the basis of this dissatisfaction in 1906. It accepted the "formulae of unity" (the three classic Reformed confessional documents) as its foundation and set itself to the task of spreading the "Reformed [*gereformeerde*] principles" contained in the confessions. The word *gereformeerde* was chosen consciously to indicate that one did not want to cede this word to the newly formed *Gereformeerde* Churches in the Netherlands as a particular church body.

[3]   Or "Reformed League." We shall leave the name, *Gereformeerde Bond*, untranslated. It continues to play a significant role in the life of the church, and its name, *gereformeerde*, reflects its self-understanding as a champion of the old Reformed faith.

The full name was originally "Gereformeerde Bond for the Liberation of the Netherlands Reformed Church." The word "liberation" meant the abolishment of the organization of the church essentially in place since 1816, which had been instituted by the state, in order that the church could again be itself. Then, specifically, local congregations would be given freedom to organize themselves.

This same freedom would also exist for the differing groups within the church, or so one of the initiators, Hugo Visscher (1864-1947), advanced. In any case that would be so for those of a *gereformeerde* disposition. Thus these differing groups would be able to live together within the Reformed Church, which would henceforth be nothing more than an administrative whole. In that connection, Visscher talked about a "modus vivendi." On mutual arrangement a "separation of property" could take place by means of which ecclesiastical property would be divided among the various groups.

In the meantime then, those of a *gereformeerde* disposition would be able to advocate for what Visscher called "the reconstruction of the *gereformeerde* church." A "reborn *Gereformeerde* Church" was accepted as the official goal in the group's by-laws. In any case, it is thereby stated unambiguously that the existing Reformed Church was no longer seen as truly "*Gereformeerde*."

However, this course, which had been chosen at the outset, evoked discord among the members of the new *Gereformeerde Bond*. Many of them found that the "modus vivendi"-ideal that Visscher advocated looked too much like the *Doleantie*—to separate itself from the church as a whole to be able to go one's own way. A separation was precisely what was not wanted.

In 1909, under the leadership of M. van Grieken, it was decided to make a change in course as well as to change the name. The thought of "liberating" the Reformed Church from its existing synodical organization and thereafter to work toward a "modus vivendi" was abandoned as a goal. The name chosen was "*Gereformeerde Bond* for the spread and defense of the Truth in the Netherlands Reformed (*Gereformeerde*) Church." Thereby, what was positively intended stood at the center.

It was thus stated implicitly that one wished to continue to belong to the Netherlands Reformed Church. That was all the more strongly expressed in the fact that in the new articulation of its goal, the word "*gereformeerde*" was added as further qualification between parentheses in the name of this church: "Netherlands Reformed (*Gereformeerde*)

Church." It again appears that the name, *gereformeerde*, was not ceded to the *dolerenden*. Indeed, differently from in 1906, it was maintained as a starting point that the Netherlands Reformed Church was itself, *in principle*, still a *gereformeerde* church, and had always been so.

That, in the judgment of the *Gereformeerde Bond*, this church was *in fact* no (longer) so, was equally emphasized. The "*Gereformeerde* Truth" would have to be spread and defended anew. So it was hoped to attain what had been stated in its by-laws: "the establishment of the Reformed Church from its deep fall."

In 1909, it was also decided to publish its own weekly newspaper, *De Waarheidsvriend*.[4] It still appears as the weekly organ of the *Gereformeerde Bond* under the same name. The by-laws of the *Bond* have remained unchanged since 1909.

In the congregations where one feels oneself connected with the *Gereformeerde Bond*, a very particular type of faith experience has developed. There one finds a strong emphasis on God's holiness and sovereignty, and, in contradistinction, the smallness and sinfulness of the human. One recognizes these notions in the psalms. In church services of the *Gereformeerde Bond*, the psalms alone (set in strophes) are sung. The conviction that the salvation of every person depends on God's free election is deeply experienced. One finds support for that conviction in the confessional documents, in particular the Canons of Dort.

That one belongs to the elect (and not to the rejected) is clearly not self-evident to the "Bonders." One can experience the certainty of election only in one's own heart. That is the "experience" that stands at the center of the life of faith for the Bonders. In that way the *Gereformeerde Bond* is, as is the *Reveil*, a continuation or renascence of the "Further Reformation" of the seventeenth and eighteenth centuries.

It is difficult to give a summary expression of the life of faith within the circle of the *Gereformeerde Bond*. The *Bond* is, despite its strict principles, not a unity among mutuals. The internal opposition that existed from its origins has never completely disappeared. There has always remained a certain tension between those who, on the one side, oriented themselves fully to the Netherlands Reformed Church, and on the other side, those who sought their continued spiritual existence in their own circle. We shall return to this tension in the following chapter.

4   "The Friend of the Truth."

The Union of Liberal Reformed

That a mutual difference of opinion would exist among the liberals is, of course, less surprising, having seen that they cherished an emphasis on freedom of conviction. At the end of the nineteenth century, optimism and the self-assuredness by which the "modern" ideas had been brought forward, suffered reversal and became disappointments instead. These modern ideas appeared to have less power to convince than had been expected. Was not reality more unmanageable than one could ever, by oneself, posit within a closed system of thought?

Some pled for a new way of thinking, one that emerged not from the unity of God and the human, but from the duality between the two. Between God and the human, God and the world, a chasm opens, it began to be said, a chasm which must be bridged from God's side and which God *has* bridged, in Christ. In this context, liberals should no longer be anxious in speaking of "sin" and "grace." Cherished ideas that had been worked out in orthodox circles, such as "reconciliation through the blood of Christ," were certainly found to be too dogmatic. Still, there was now more receptivity here for Christ as Savior.

Pioneers in this way of thinking were the Leiden professors Karel Hendrik Roessingh (1886-1925), Gerrit Jan Heering (1879-1955), and Hendrik Tjakko de Graaf (1875-1930). The two first named belonged to the Remonstrance Brotherhood, but they had a good deal of influence among young Reformed liberals.

Accompanying this new theological orientation was a new view of the meaning of the church. There originated with Reformed liberals a need for an organizational way to accent their place in the Reformed Church. This was all the more urgent because the legitimacy of that place had been attacked continually from the orthodox side. The Netherlands Protestant Covenant, established in 1870, with its antichurch policy, could no longer suffice. Thus their own organization emerged. The Union of Liberal Reformed was established in 1913. The weekly paper, *Kerk en Wereld*,[5] functioned as its organ. In 1995 that paper evolved into *Vrij Zicht*,[6] a common publication of various liberal Protestant organizations.

The Union positioned itself contentiously where party conflicts made battle necessary. But its real goal was not to turn itself against others. It was and is more positive: that there be space for a pluriformity

---

[5]   "Church and World."
[6]   "Free View."

of belief and experience of faith within the Netherlands Reformed Church.

Liberals greatly value faith experience that is open to modern culture and the results of modern science.

The Twentieth Century: Increasing Numbers of Unchurched

As we saw at the beginning of the first chapter, about half of the Dutch population still belonged to the Netherlands Reformed Church at the beginning of the twentieth century. The percentage of Reformed, according the various censuses between 1849 and 1879, remained at about the same level (54.5 per cent); it had declined in 1889 to 48.7 per cent but only as a consequence of the *Doleantie*. In 1899 only a small decline was ascertained—the percentage was then 48.4.

From that point, censuses disclose a genuine decline—an average of nearly five percent every ten years. In 1930 the Reformed Church only included about a third of the Dutch population (then nearly eight million residents), or 34.5 percent.

In the same period, the percentage of those who belonged to no church rose accordingly—from 2.3 percent in 1899 to 14.4 percent in 1930. It can be concluded from these numbers that this rise had occurred almost completely at the expense of Reformed membership.

This development is not to be seen apart from intervening events of the first decades of the twentieth century. The First World War raged from 1914 to 1918. It is true that the Netherlands remained neutral, but it still experienced major economic consequences from the war. Further, growing industry brought with it a process of urbanization. More and more people left the small communal villages where everyone knew everyone else and crowded into the anonymity of urban social life.

At the end of the 1920s an international economic crisis occurred, and, consequently, great unemployment. In precisely those years, between 1920 and 1930, the decline of the percentage of Reformed and the rise in the percentage of those who belonged to no church were spectacular. Again, both in almost the same measure, apparently corresponding with each other—about seven percent.

Those who filled leadership positions within the Reformed Church belonged in general to the upper stratum of society, or at least in the middle groups (employers, members of the middle class). That contributed to the estrangement of the working population from the church. That estrangement was aggravated by the indifference of the official church to the social question. Socialism had already emerged in the nineteenth century, but, in general, ecclesiastical reaction to it was only negative or defensive.

Struggle for Church Renewal: *Kerkherstel*[7] and *Kerkopbouw*

The Netherlands Reformed Church had become a house divided against itself, rent by party conflict. It had fallen into (at least) four different groups, each with its own organization. The intolerability of this situation began to become clear even to the synod.

It was the confessionals in particular who, in the line of Hoedemaker, continued to advocate strongly for the restoration [*herstel*], or reorganization, of the church. Their leader was the Groningen professor Theodorus Lambertus Haitjema (1888-1972). At their urging, the synod instituted a small commission for reorganization under Haitjema's chairmanship.

In 1929, this commission did indeed introduce a proposal for a new *Algemeen Reglement*. It was proposed that a new synod would emerge, consisting of representatives of the classes (one per classis). This synod would not only have a greater size than the existing synod, but would also have a broader task. It would be more than administrative; it would also offer spiritual leadership. Classical gatherings would also be reinstated as gatherings of the offices. And a clear description of what is meant by the "doctrine of the church" should be given. Maintenance of the confession should be taken seriously, including, if necessary, the practice of ecclesiastical discipline in matters of doctrine.

The synod rejected this proposal in its 1930 session by the smallest possible majority, ten votes to nine. In reaction to the decision, Haitjema and his supporters established the "Netherlands Reformed Covenant for the Restoration of the Church [*Kerkherstel*]." Confessionals and members of the *Gereformeerde Bond* joined forces in this new body. A number of ethicals joined as well. A certain zealousness for reorganization in the spirit of the 1929 proposal remained, with as yet no result.

However, party differences continued to do their work. In 1931, the "Union for the Building Up of the Church [*Kerkopbouw*]" was established in opposition to *Kerkherstel*. It was made up primarily of liberals and ethicals who sought a church renewal that embraced

---

[7]   *Kerkherstel*, or the "restoration of the Church," and *Kerkopbouw*, the "building up of the church."

much more than reorganization. *Kerkopbouw* accented the necessity of contemporary confession more than the formal maintenance of the classic confession in itself. *Kerkherstel*'s plans were viewed as having focused too much on the reinstatement of the previous order and as being too little open to the future. An important role in *Kerkopbouw* was played by Oepke Noordmans (1871-1956), a minister in Laren in the province of Gelderland since 1923. Noordmans would also practice enormous influence on further developments in the Netherlands Reformed Church.

In 1934, *Kerkopbouw* introduced its own proposal for a new *Algemeen Reglement* with the synod. In 1935, the synod also rejected this proposal. That led to the emergence of a conversation between *Kerkherstel* and *Kerkopbouw*, and they found common ground in a mutual proposal. It was offered to the synod in 1937.

The synod gathering was observed with great anticipation. With the acceptance of a proposal with such broad support, it could actually succeed in transcending party conflict. However, that did not happen. After extensive discussions, first in the synod and afterwards in classical gatherings and provincial ecclesiastical administrations, the proposal was finally definitively rejected August 8, 1939. The fear that the proposed reorganization would lead to doctrinal discipline won out over the longing for church renewal.

Less than a month after the synod's decision, the Second World War broke out. This time the Netherlands would become involved in the war. It was precisely through the emergency situation of German occupation that the barriers to renewal in the Reformed Church could be demolished. We shall speak of that in the following chapter.

CHAPTER 8

After 1940: The New Course of the Apostolate

On May 10, 1940, the Second World War, which had broken out September 1, 1939, reached the Netherlands. The years of German occupation were a period of confrontation with the ideology of National Socialism. This ideology would push to assert itself ever more forcefully. It would find primary expression in measures intended to discriminate against and deport Jews.

National Socialism was a glorification of a particular (Germanic) people and race, of a peculiar "blood and soil." In Germany, one appealed to God the Creator and to God's providential leading, which were considered evident in particular successes in the first years of the war. Adolf Hitler, the German Reichschancellor, was viewed as the Fuhrer whom God had sent to lead the German people.

Thus National Socialism could cohere with Christian terminology while at the same time reverting to pre-Christian German paganism with its myths and motifs. The Germanic or "Arian" race was considered legitimately superior and so would have to be "purely" maintained. The destruction of the entire European Jewish world was a necessary condition in the attainment of that goal. Oppression of Jews was not a secondary matter for National Socialism but its main task.

The Synod Moved to Confession

Under these circumstances, the Netherlands Reformed Church also faced absolutely new challenges. On May 10, 1940, intra-ecclesiastical party conflicts were relegated to a lower status. Other matters became more important. Measures taken by the German occupier would again and again force the Reformed Church to take a public position. This would result in unambiguous protests in the name of the synod. These protests would simply and directly appear to have the character of a confession when directed against a strange ideology.

Powerful leadership was given by the Reverend Koeno Henricus Eikelhoff Gravemeyer (1883-1970), from the Hague, who had become secretary of the synod on April 1, 1940. A steadfast and intrepid man, he was the right man in the right place for the Reformed Church at this time.

At his urging, the General Synodical Commission (i.e. the executive committee of the synod) took the initiative in the formation of the "Convent of Churches" already on June 25, 1940, the aim of which would be to determine a common course of action to be followed. In this Convent, later to be called the "Interchurch Consultation," seven other Protestant church bodies (including the Reformed Churches in the Netherlands) were represented along with the Netherlands Reformed Church. After the end of 1941, a regular consultation with the Roman Catholic Church in the Netherlands also took place. Gravemeyer was its secretary. The Interchurch Consultation protested repeatedly against certain measures taken by the occupier—by letter, by telegram, and at times through an audience with the Reichscommissioner Dr. A. Seyss Inquart (head of the German occupation authority). That happened for the first time (by letter) October 24, 1940. At issue was discrimination against Jews. This discrimination would manifest itself ever more blatantly. The longer it continued, the more it would take on the character of persecution. The churches reacted against this, not only because it was "in conflict with Christian mercy," nor only because there were Jewish Christians among those affected, but above all because the Jewish people as a whole is "the people" "from which the Savior of the world is born."

The Interchurch Consultation also objected to the way in which the occupiers attempted to propagate the ideas of National Socialism with the Dutch population (which happened in part through measures concerning the organization of education and the organization of a "ministry of labor"). The arbitrary nature of the occupier's activity was exposed repeatedly, as was the denial of rights to which Dutch citizens, particularly Jews, were subjected.

Local congregations were informed regularly of the mutual protest by the churches through messages delivered from pulpits. In general, the protests were fruitless. But the fact that they took place was very significant, and certainly they did not leave the occupiers cold. The messages from the pulpit, in particular, were a thorn in their eye.

In particular cases, what happened during church services resulted in intervention by the occupying power. A Sunday churchgoer could easily hear a clear statement in a particular sermon or prayer that could in turn be passed on to the Germans and subsequently become the occasion for the arrest of that minister. Many Reformed ministers spent shorter or longer times in prison. Some of the ministers who had been arrested did not survive their imprisonment. The secretary of the synod, Gravemeyer, was imprisoned from May to December, 1940. He was seen by the German authorities as the soul of the church resistance.

Twice during the occupation, the Reformed synod found itself forced to send a pastoral letter to members of the congregations. It was especially on the second of these occasions, in the fall of 1942, that information was given concerning the struggle that must be waged against National Socialism as a way of life and a worldview. That letter was sent by ecclesiastical couriers to church councils. Open publication was deemed too dangerous. For this reason, many church councils unfortunately remained ignorant of the letter.

When the tide of the war began to turn in 1943, the attitude and the strategy of the German occupiers changed. Thus far they had worn a mask of good will; now they let it drop. They were ever more prepared to press people into service as workers in German industry or in the construction of defense works. Many hid. Others resisted. Church protests continued to sound. Many ministers, church councils, and congregational members quietly offered help to refugees and those in hiding, Jewish persons included. That was, of course, extremely risky, and many who offered help fell victim in turn.

During the time of the hunger winter, 1944-1945, the entire emphasis of church work was centered on the ability to organize emergency food provisions with the help of farmers and shippers.

The 'Commission for Ecclesiastical Consultation': Hendrik Kraemer

The need and the press of the occupation evoked an expectation of synodical leadership from across the entire Reformed Church. It was understood how important it was for the church to act together and to hold to a common course of action.

And a central leadership existed and offered advice. It is true that this leadership was not always as clear and courageous as some desired. Views on which policy to follow, on questions of what was principally commanded or practically wise, diverged in synodical circles.

In any case, the synod began to function as had not been thought possible before, and in a manner that had not been foreseen at all by the church order. Need broke law.

This development was furthered by the fact that from the beginning of the occupation, the synod looked to special advisory bodies for assistance. That too was new. At the invitation of the synod, eighteen prominent church members convened on August 27, 1940, for the first gathering of what would be called the Commission for Ecclesiastical Consultation. Those invited were theologians, ministers, and congregational members (laity) from the various groups within the church.

The proposal for the gathering of this sort of commission had its origin with Hendrik Kraemer (1888-1965), a professor at Leiden and previously in missionary service in Indonesia. He had made the proposal a few months before the German invasion as a means by which the church would be able to break through the tradition of silence that had long existed when it came to the burning questions of the day. He had himself witnessed how the Indonesian church had achieved church renewal and the uncoupling of the bond between the church and colonial government. The convocation of a "great gathering" of office-bearers and laity had immediately tapped the power of being church that had remained latent for so long. Kraemer hoped that something similar could also happen in the Netherlands Reformed Church. In the crisis of the occupation, such a move was more urgent and more necessary than ever before.

At the gathering of August 27, 1940, Kraemer himself acted as spokesman. He emphasized the peculiar nature of the church—that it has a task from God on behalf of the world, an "apostolic" task. He also emphasized the shameful weakness of the church, the fact that it was scarcely equipped for its task. This equipping, he said, must immediately be undertaken. Specifically, work must be done to mobilize and activate members of the congregations. Congregations would have to function as true communions, refuges for the attacked, the persecuted, and the oppressed.

Kraemer's call made an impact. It was decided to form a number of working groups to offer advice in different areas. Among others there emerged, under the leadership of Kraemer himself, the work group, "Church and the strengthening of congregations" [*Gemeeteopbouw*].

The Lunteren Circle

Within the structure of work groups just formed, a number of younger ministers, who had been impressed even prior to the Second World War by the necessity for a new way of thinking of church and faith, had begun to collaborate. They had established contact with congenial spirits in Germany, where the church had, of course, been confronted with the challenge of National Socialism earlier than in the Netherlands. At the outset of the occupation they had formed what would henceforth be called the "Lunteren Circle" (after the place where they held their first gathering August 22, 1940). The initiator was the Amsterdam minister, Jan Koopmans (1905-1945).

The insights of the theologian Karl Barth (1886-1968) particularly inspired them. Barth had played a leading role in the German church conflict. His conviction that the will of God is not to be derived from the course of events (not, for example, from success) and also not from natural realities (such as people or race), but exclusively from the Bible as witness of Jesus Christ, made him a radical, principled opponent of the ideology of National Socialism and a powerful advocate of the freedom and the peculiarity of the church in view of the state. He had articulated concisely that conviction, with its consequences, in six theses accepted at a German ecclesiastical gathering in 1934 (well known since then as the Barmen Theses). Shortly thereafter, the German authorities expelled Barth as an undesirable alien. However, he remained involved in events in Germany from Switzerland.

One of the participants in the Lunteren Circle was the Amsterdam minister and later professor at Leiden, Kornelis Heiko Miskotte (1894-1976). He had been one of the first to advance the notion that Judaism is more than a preparatory phase (subsequently bypassed) for Christianity; that it must, rather, be taken seriously as a religion that stands on its own with its own value and meaning. In October 1939, he had published his book, *Edda and Thora*. In that book, he had shown how the ancient Germanic religion (*Edda*, now repristinated in National Socialism) is diametrically opposed to the religion of Israel (*Thora*, the Old Testament). He had thereby indicated as well the essential relationship of Christian belief with that of Israel. These insights had become particularly relevant after the German invasion of the Netherlands.

From the Lunteren Circle, the synod was again and again encouraged to take a stronger, more courageous position (and criticized for its inaction). Unofficial ecclesiastical resistance had united in this circle.

At various times the Lunteren Circle drafted and distributed its own illegal documents. Of primary importance was a document that was formulated in the form of a confession of faith, under the title, *Wat wij wel en wat we niet gelooven*[1] in 1941. It was strongly inspired by the Barmen Theses, but it made explicit what had still remained implicit in these theses—the unacceptability of anti-Semitism, and that from the confession of the election of Israel (still and always in effect). The drafters (who included Koopmans and Miskotte) hoped that the synod would officially accept the document. Alas, that did not happen.

But as has been said, different members of the Lunteren Circle became involved in the work group structure instituted by the synod. In that way the stimulation of this circle found its way into official church policy.

Church and *Gemeenteopbouw* [2]

That the internal party conflict had been relegated to second place in one blow after May 10, 1940, did not mean that the reorganization of the church had been taken off the agenda. In contrast to 1938, however, it was understood that some such reorganization would have a chance of success only if the congregations and church councils themselves could come to an understanding of the church. First of all, one must learn to be the church together at the grassroots level and enter discussion with one another beyond party divisions. Of first importance, one must learn that "being the church" means "being the church in mission." Where the missionary ("apostolic") task is commonly grasped, just there a mutual discussion of the confession comes into view.

This was the starting point and the agenda of the work group, Church and *Gemeenteopbouw*. It is important to note that representatives of nearly every church party were members of this work group (only

---

[1]   "What we believe and what we do not believe."
[2]   *Gemeenteopbouw* can be translated as "congregational education." However, the awkwardness of that phrase in English coupled with the importance of this body in the life of the NHK suggest leaving the word untranslated.

the *Gereformeerde Bond* was not represented). Matters were dealt with energetically. Preparatory materials were gathered. Delegates from the work group visited every classis gathering (which met in special session for that reason in January 1941). Church councils were also visited. Similar rounds of visits took place later.

Particular thought was given to the fact that in many places besides (and in opposition to) the "official" Reformed congregations, special (liberal as well as orthodox) "evangelical gatherings"[3] had originated. These were unions that had, without ecclesiastical status, organized their own church services, of a different party than that of the "official" church. This state of affairs, in which the existence of congregations and an "evangelical gathering" stood side by side as organizations, was the way in which the party question had been worked out practically in the Reformed Church.

Church and *Gemeenteopbouw* worked diligently where possible to bring about mutual contact. That contact would have to be present (as put in words prepared by Kraemer) "in obedience to Holy Scripture and on the soil of the confessional documents." The intention was to attain a situation in which the work of the "evangelical gatherings" would be recognized by the relevant church councils as church work, at least insofar as that church council understood itself in a shared pastoral responsibility for that work. That goal, however, was not reached in many cases.

Gradually, Church and *Gemeenteopbouw* shifted its work to a more direct promotion of discussion between the parties. At the request of the work group, Miskotte drafted a short text that was accepted at a large conference organized by Church and *Gemeenteopbouw* in Doorn in 1943. It was to be the starting point and guideline for that discussion. The document was circulated under the title, *Wij gelooven en belijden*.[4]

Here as well, the influence of Barth's thought comes through. The central points of the Christian faith are articulated in seven theses. Belief in Jesus Christ is the starting point and the central point. The church, so it is said, lives from him: "to trust in him and to obey him is the true Christian confession." The significance of Jesus Christ is set out in a discussion of the various aspects of his work—priestly, prophetic,

---

[3] *Evangelaties.* Unofficial gatherings of worship or prayer whereby believers of like minds could gather outside official approval of the local church council.

[4] "We believe and confess." These are sometimes known as the *Doornse theses.*

and royal. The whole of humanity (as borne in God's patience) is further discussed, as well as the nature of the church and what may be expected—the "kingdom of God," the "completion."

An extensive explanation, from the hand of the Zeist minister Hendrikus Berkhof (1914-1995), indicated the intention of the document. Those who would discuss the document would, it was hoped, discover two things:

> First, that the church is larger than our party....And second, the church has borders. There are ideas that cannot be brought into agreement with Christ and the Scripture....We must thus break with them, or we must break with the church.

The work of Church and *Gemeenteopbouw* continued after the war. In the final months before the end of the war, it was not possible to maintain contact between the synodical center in The Hague (in the western part of the country still under occupation) and the parts of the nations that had already been liberated. Directly following the German capitulation in June and July, 1945, Gravemeyer, Kraemer, and the religious socialist Willem Banning (1888-1971) undertook a long journey in the areas above the great rivers. The goal was to reestablish contact between the synodical center and the church in the nation and to take up the thread of *Gemeenteopbouw* once again. The three represented the breadth of the Reformed Church: Gravemeyer from the confessional circle, Kraemer related to the ethical party, and Banning as representative of the liberals.

The Work Order: Preparation for a Genuine General Synod

Proponents of reorganization of the church had discovered one more thing since 1938. They had understood that one must not attempt to achieve the entire reorganization at once, but must work step by step. The synod as well was now prepared to move ahead by means of steps.

In 1942, it installed a commission which was given the task of proposing a "work order," a transitional set of regulations. This would, then, make possible the calling of a broad "general synod," a new style of synod, which could emerge as a true representative of the entire church. The breadth of the Reformed Church was represented in the commission, this time including the *Gereformeerde Bond*.

In 1944, the commission was ready to present its proposals. In July of that year, they were accepted by the synod. Before the actual introduction of the proposal, it was still required that at least two-thirds of the total number of members of all the provincial ecclesiastical administrations agree. Because of war conditions, final approval took place in July 1945. The two-thirds minimum was easily passed; only two of the sixty-four members of the provincial ecclesiastical administrations voted against the proposal.

Thus eight proposed work-order articles were accepted as "additional articles" to those of the *Algemeen Reglement*. It was determined by these articles that the Netherlands Reformed Church would indeed gather "in General Synod." It was now stated in so many words that this synod would conduct its tasks "in obedience to Holy Scripture and standing on the soil of the confessional documents" (this formulation repeated here). The synod would completely replace the old administrative synod.

The first task given the synod was the preparation and establishment of a church order to replace the *Algemeen Reglement*. The synod would also have as its task "to witness, with the Church in all its parts, to the Gospel of Jesus Christ before government and people." This last phrase formalized what had in fact been practiced in the time of the occupation.

The new general synod would consist of representatives from the classical gatherings, one from each classis, forty-five altogether (thirty ministers, fifteen elders). Thereby, one important element of the Dort Church Order was reestablished with honor.

The End of the Administrative Church

On the basis of the work order, a new general synod convened for its first gathering October 31, 1945, in the New Church in Amsterdam. In a prayer service, held beforehand on October 30, Miskotte pithily articulated the historic moment. He began his sermon by citing the prescription of the Dort Church order of 1619 that had never been executed: that a national (general) synod must take place (at least) once every three years. And he stated: "Not after three years, but after three centuries, the envisioned general synod gathers."

The new synod quickly commissioned the preparation of a new church order that would completely replace the *Algemeen Reglement*. The broad commission that was named for this purpose consisted, like its predecessor, of representatives from all parties and movements within the Reformed Church.

Already by 1947, the commission could present its proposed church order to the synod. After a number of rounds of discussion and amendments, the final approval by the synod (consisting of double the usual number) took place December 7, 1950. The proposal was accepted by a large majority. Only fourteen of the ninety synod members declared themselves against the proposal.

On May 1, 1951, the new church order became effective. However much it has been amended since that time, it has remained as the church order in its basic structure. This structure is included in thirty articles. Twenty "ordinances" embrace accompanying regulations that implement the basic church order.

The fact that the Netherlands Reformed Church has established and introduced its own new church order is itself of great significance. The *Gereformeerde* churches that had emerged from the *Doleantie* realized the reestablishment of the church by a return to the Dort Church Order. The Reformed Church sought and reached it by a different route.

Fundamental elements of the established ecclesiastical structure of the new church order have indeed been derived from the Dort Church Order. That is specifically the case in the reestablishment of the gatherings of offices of the church at its various levels: regional (by classis) and provincial. Classical gatherings received again their old, full authority. The former "provincial synods" returned under the name of "provincial church gatherings" (and were included more fully in the whole of the national church). The general synod as a gathering of offices had been reintroduced, in fact, already in 1945, with the acceptance of the work order (henceforth half its number would consist of ministers, and half from the other office-bearers).

The various changes meant a definitive repeal of the administrative structure introduced in 1816. There still remained administrative bodies (executive committees), of course, but they functioned only in service of the gatherings of the offices. Those gatherings bore the final responsibility.

Still, this church order is not a repristination of the church order of Dort. What is new is that the Netherlands Reformed Church presents itself as a "Christ confessing *volkskerk*" (as Haitjema, one of the drafters of the new church order, put it so strikingly). By that it is said that it understands itself—always and ever renewed—in covenant with and related to the entire (Dutch) people. That stance has a historical and a principled background. A new understanding of the missionary calling in a secularized (unchurched) society appears. But that understanding coheres with the way in which this church had been rooted in the birth and the existence of the Dutch nation from its beginning.

The New Church Order (1): The Reformed Church as a *Volkskerk*

We will examine this last matter somewhat further.

The character of the Reformed Church as a *volkskerk* came under discussion in the first, introductory chapter above. There we saw that in Article II of the church order "birth members" ("those born of Reformed parents") were accounted for as well as "confessing members" and "baptized members" in the membership lists of the Reformed Church. There was no such provision in the Dort Church Order. It was present in the *Algemeen Reglement* (as it was amended in 1852).

The clause, "those born of Reformed parents," was certainly not intended to mean "membership by virtue of birth." Article II speaks of a membership "by virtue of the covenant of grace" (a definition not included in the *Algemeen Reglement*). But this covenant (God's covenant) is assuredly seen as genuinely far-reaching, including both parents and children. Illustrative of this is the note set in the *Algemeen Reglement* at this notion of "birth members":

> The Church extends as far as possible its notion of those who must be counted as members of the congregation, because it wants to embrace as much as possible, all those who have not expressly stated that they do not want to belong to it, in order that by its influence it may be a blessing to many as possible.

The New Church Order (2): The Apostolate

As has been said, the character of the Reformed Church as a *volkskerk* specifically includes a missionary aspect. That aspect emerges in Article VIII, concerning "the apostolate of the church." The previous articles deal with the church as such: what it is, who belong to it, how it is structured and organized. From Article VIII on, the life and work of the church are articulated. It is striking that the apostolate is mentioned first among these latter articles.

The word "apostolate" points to the apostles in the New Testament, sent out by Jesus to proclaim the gospel of God's reign by word and deed. The Reformed Church now understands itself to stand within this same "apostolic" task. The manner in which this is stated here in Article VIII is striking; the church understands itself "set as a

Christ-confessing communion of faith in the world to bear witness to God's promises and commands for all people and powers."

The apostolate stands at the center of the church order. It is with this in mind that a place is given here, for example, to the "assisting bodies"[5] of the general synod (and other gatherings of the offices). Such institutions for help and advice must exist, according to Article VI-1, "when the responsibility for the ministry of the Church on the different areas of life demands it." "Ministry" thus involves more than internal church life. Indeed, directly after the war, various "councils" had already been established (as successors of the work group structure that had been given life by the synod at the outset of the occupation). A number of different councils were given express tasks that turned outward.

The apostolate as "bearing witness" to "God's promises and commands for all humans and powers" must not only play itself out in mission work far away. In Article VIII, it is emphatically involved in the particular, Dutch society as well. Two matters are spoken of in that connection: first, "spreading of the gospel" among "those who have been estranged from it"; second, "continuing work for the christianizing[6] of the life of the people." It is said of that:

> The Church...turns itself, in expectation of the reign of God, in the work of Christianizing to the government and the people, to point life to God's promises and commands.

Here there appears to be a different relation between church and government from that which was found in the Dort Church Order. There we saw how a place was left for a continuing governmental influence, for direct governmental involvement in church matters. There is no more mention of this in the new church order. The church knows itself to be free over and against the government; the church is prepared to address it even critically when necessary (appealing to "God's promises and commands"). In the following chapter we will see how this was made concrete in the period following 1951.

Directly following the article on the apostolate is the article on youth work (IX). The missionary, apostolic theme strikes there as well. The church's task is, it states, "to cooperate in the formation of

---

5   *Organen van bijstand*, literally, "organs for assistance." These were very important bodies in the new church order that function rather like agencies in an American church.

6   *Kerstening* or "making Christian."

the youth." And this is not only about the youth of the church. The church understands itself "jointly responsible for the upbringing and the education of the youth of the entire nation in family and school, in order that obedience to God's commands takes shape here as well."

The New Church Order (3): Conversation with Israel.

Yet another element from the article on the apostolate (VIII) invites reflection. In connection with the apostolate, another concrete task of the church is identified: "conversation with Israel." In fact, that task is of primary consideration in the summation of the tasks of the church. The relation of the church to the Jewish people is thereby acknowledged as unique and as fundamental for the entire of the missionary stance of the church as it turns outward.

It is important that this relation is typified by the word "conversation." Talk of a "mission" to the Jews is expressly avoided. For the church, Israel is not purely the recipient of its message; it is its partner in discussion. Or at least when Israel itself *wants* to be so. It can certainly have reasons *not* to so desire! Were not Jews often the target of persecution by the Christians, by the church? A discussion, a dialogue, can finally only be advanced when both partners are prepared to engage. Such a discussion presupposes mutual openness to the contribution of the other. In its relation to Israel, the church must not only want to *speak*; it must also, and first of all, be willing to listen.

These last considerations are not expressed literally in the article of the church order under discussion. But they are presupposed in the proper use of the term "conversation." They are to be read between the lines. All the more so now, since an amendment to the text, brought in 1991, expressly states that the "church *seeks* conversation with Israel."

The experience of the Second World War finds a place in this cautious description of the relation between the church and Israel. Already years prior to the beginning of the war, Miskotte, a pioneer in this area, advanced the notion that this relation is of a unique sort. But we saw how the Reformed Church, together with the other Dutch churches, was forced by the persecution of the Jews under its very eyes during the time of the German occupation, to give witness to its connection with the Jewish people. The churches' understanding of that relation had suddenly emerged. It had been a shock to become conscious of the Jewish provenance and character of the Bible, and of the continuing, unique place in God's intentions that extend to the Jewish people, even within the New Testament. That notion was retained following the war. The Reformed Church has brought it to expression in its new church order.

The New Church Order (4): Confessing and Confession

After the apostolate of the church is dealt with so extensively, and thus in the same context, the confession of the church comes under discussion in the church order. Article X handles that matter.

The question of how the Reformed Church relates to the classic Reformed confessional documents had been on the agenda continually since the nineteenth century. We saw that the question had never been answered officially by the synod. We also saw how the beginning of an answer began to shimmer through precisely during the time of the occupation in the formulation that the church (the general synod) will do its work "in obedience to Holy Scripture and standing on the soil of the confessional documents." In Article X of the new church order, that is further elaborated and articulated. The phrase, "standing on the soil of the confessional documents," is replaced here by, "in communion with the confession of the fathers."

This last formulation had been the object of much discussion. It was deemed to be too vague, particularly by the right wing (the *Gereformeerde Bond*). Instead of "in communion with" they argued for "in agreement with." At the least, that would have to be added. Only then could there be talk of a genuine bond with the confessional documents. However, this plea found no hearing with the majority of the synod. That was even less the case with protests from the opposite side, the liberal side, where some had difficulty with the reference to "the confession of the fathers" as too emphatic.

It is to be noted that Article X consciously talks not about the confession but about the "confessing of the church." "Confessing" is something current, something that must ever happen anew. The church "confesses...always afresh...Jesus Christ as Head of the Church and Lord of the world," is how it is put. And confessing as a contemporary action is presupposed to be something other than a pure repetition of what was said at an earlier time. The truth cannot, so the thought that lies behind this notion, be fixed exhaustively in *one* particular confessional formula, no matter how classic. It must always be advanced anew, in new situations, in the face of new challenges. That too is articulated in Article X in the definition that the church confesses "in understanding of its responsibility for the present."

For just that reason, it cannot be said that new confession happens "in agreement with the confession of the fathers." The word "communion" offers precisely what is at issue: the essential connection with (the confession of) the forbears that nevertheless does not—decidedly not—discharge the present generation from its peculiar responsibility to say confessingly what *now* must be said.

Influences: Hoedemaker, the Ethicals, Kohlbrugge, Barth

We see various influences from the past converging in the new church order. The first of these is Hoedemaker. His considerations echo in the notion of the covenant of grace that embraces parents and children as the foundation for church membership, and in the definitions concerning the apostolic relationship of the church to government and the people. What Hoedemaker had envisioned was powerfully advanced in the commission for the proposal by Haitjema and by his student, later professor at Utrecht, Arnold Albert van Ruler (1908-1970). The latter, above all, had played an important role in the drafting of the new church order.

Moreover, we encounter ideas that already had been recommended from the "ethical" party, and through someone like Noordmans. We recognize these notions in the way in which the church order speaks of "confessing" and "confession," of "confessing" as a living matter.

Again someone must be identified here whose name arose earlier in this chapter: Barth. He emphasized in his theology the absolute otherness of God, which results in the fact that humans cannot know God on the basis of our humanity; thus we only know God because God has given God's self to us in Jesus Christ to be known. That position implies a radical critique of a liberalism that continued happily to rely on the "enlightened" or "religious" human. But it implies an equally radical critique of an orthodoxy that thought it had God's revealed truth at its disposal in confession or dogma, and was required only to "defend" or "maintain" it.

In Barth's position, one can recognize traces of Kohlbrugge's ideas, who did not allow himself to be caught in the dilemma between liberalism and orthodoxy, but instead advanced what he thought was the key issue in the church: objective, valid, salvation in Christ that transcends everything.

It was Barth's peculiar new theological initiative that had contributed decisively to the new course of the Netherlands Reformed Church and that had put the church in a position to advance beyond internal party conflicts born of the nineteenth century through its church order, effective in 1951.

That and how the developments after 1951 proceeded we shall observe in the following chapter.

CHAPTER 9

Apostolate and Confessing in the First Decades after the War

By itself, a church order does not guarantee church renewal. For that matter, it is not necessarily the case that the church order comes first and church life follows. At the very least, a mutual exchange takes place, much like the relation between legislation and society.

As we have seen, the new church order of the Netherlands Reformed Church did not appear out of nowhere. It was the fruit of a church renewal that had begun to blossom during the war. The notions embodied in the church order were already dominant in Reformed Church life from 1945 on. Sometimes they even led to initiatives that reached further than were legitimate according to the church order, strictly taken.

Church and World

The Reformed Church wanted to take its apostolic task seriously, including its place in Dutch society. Characteristic of that attitude was the foundation of the institute Church and World, established in Driebergen in November 1945.

This institute became the center for the education of church "lay" coworkers, for the work of evangelization, and for reflection on the contemporary meaning of the gospel. The plans for the institute were developed by Johan Eijkman (1893-1945), who was active in youth evangelism in Amsterdam and connected during the war with the Ecclesiastical Consultation (he was imprisoned for about a year in Buchenwald). The Reformed general synod in its old configuration (according to the *Algemeen Reglement*) had given the green light for the institute in its gathering of July 1944.

A directorate constituted the head of the institute. It consisted of the Reverend Frans. J. Pop (1903-1987), the historian Feitse Boerwinkel (1906-1987) and the lawyer Anne Willem Kist (b. 1915), among others.

The establishment of Church and World signified something completely new. It desired that society be confronted with the gospel, but also that the reverse—to take an open stance toward society—be true as well. Theological and social subjects were taught. The theologian Berkhof and the theologian-sociologist Banning were among the first primary teachers.

In its first years, the institute exercised a great drawing power. Many, both young and old, reported for education to what was called "worker in church labor" [*werker in kerkelijke arbeid*], shortened to *wika*. They did so even without the concrete prospect of a vocation. Some would later engage in the work of evangelization, others in the pastorate for recreational activities, and still others became social workers, youth workers, or catechetical workers.

It quickly became apparent that there were not as many places within the church for these *wikas* as had been hoped in the initial wave of enthusiasm. After a number of years, the education of *wikas* was changed to an education for social work. Still later, that education became independent of Church and World and of the church. The term *wika* fell into disuse.

Evangelistic and educational work was also done by Church and World itself. The fortnightly paper, the *Open Door*, became popular and stimulated local activities in a number of congregations. A great deal of thought was given to conference work as well. This took place, for example, in reflection on the way one can be Christian in one's vocation. Through the publication of a foundational course, the institute aimed at equipping lay people for full and responsible membership in the congregation.

These and similar activities were viewed with anxiety by the right wing of the Reformed Church, specifically by the *Gereformeerde Bond*. Could what happened at Church and World stand the test of the confession? Was the biblical message not identified too closely with a (left-wing) political ideology? Conflicts with the synod would not be avoided. In later years, the institute stood at a greater distance from the church. Various activities (e.g., publication of catechetical materials) were taken over by other ecclesiastical institutions.

Christian Existence in the Society of the Netherlands

How the Reformed synod intended to remain faithful to its apostolic task as described in the church order within Dutch society was stated clearly in its publication, in 1955, of the pastoral document, *Christian existence in the society of the Netherlands.* The proposal was drafted by a commission chaired by Miskotte. Few other writings are as characteristic of the position of the Netherlands Reformed Church in the years following the war.

An unambiguous position was chosen here against the notion of "antithesis," which was propagated by Abraham Kuyper and spread widely among the *Gereformeerden.* Being Christian is not, so it was stated, the same as holding to a particular "Christian" life- or worldview, or to "Christian principles."

Being Christian in society thus does not in and of itself mean membership in a Christian organization or a Christian political party. In fact, organizations that call themselves "Christian" run the danger of thinking in contraries and of identifying obedience to Christ with its own group interest. Then the Word of God is likened to particular, relative, questionable human insights. Similar equivalencies signify a short circuit and must, said the synod, be avoided.

Being Christian, also insofar as it finds expression in the society, is described here simply as "a manner of being, a way of existence." It is "to have a Lord and then also to conform to his lordship, which includes everything." Certainly, a Christian is called to live differently, to judge differently, than one would do naturally. But this being different does "not abolish our communion with the world." Much more, it "includes" that communion "in a deep way." Thus it is not about "antithesis" but about "solidarity."

We have now no longer to do with a self-conscious, proud, Western European culture, said the synod in 1955, as had been the case in the nineteenth century. We are facing a culture in which one accepts one's coming of age as a burden and suffers existence. The attitude of the modern human is often, even unconsciously, determined by anxiety.

We Christians stand not over and against, but beside this human being. We have precisely *there, side by side* with others, the goal of living, judging, and acting differently. But, *along side of them* and thus serving them.

The Reformed synod did not intend to deny that a conflict continues between the "lordship of Christ" and the "powers of darkness." But quite differently than the proponents of the "antithesis," it also believed

> that the separation between the two at this period of time is difficult to designate and that in general they do coincide with the difference between the aspirations and organizations of Christians and non-Christians in this time....There is a subjection to the powers of the age precisely within Christian circles which hampers a way of being different. And there is a blessed unrest and uprising among non-Christians against that which is wrong, which arouses them to go new ways, of which we should not dare to say that God's good favor is absent. Christians should join in that for the sake of the common need and the new possibilities of this time.

Thus we may consider, so it was further stated, that the church is "our first and real environment." To stand in the world, to be engaged on behalf of a livable society, coheres so much with the essence of the church that

> Christian responsibility for the culture must be expressed not primarily as individual Christians accompany one another in separate organizations, but through the church itself; the same who celebrates the liturgy and fulfills the service of prayers for the need of the world.

Not all church members are societally or politically one with each other, but they need not be. The point is to distinguish well. On the one side is the faith that they confess together. On the other side are societal convictions, attitudes, and behaviors that everyone derives personally from the confession. These, however much they are derived from one and the same confession (when all is well), can be different. Church members have to respect one another in their mutual difference.

Does that not make the authority of the church powerless over its members? No, for on the one hand the Christian however much he or she is personally responsible, is not an individualist. On the other hand, the authority of the church is just there to "ensure the freedom of the believing, acting individual."

These then are some of the main ideas from the synodical pastoral document, *Christian existence in the society of the Netherlands*. The document caused a great stir, specifically in the circles of Christian organizations. The fact that the Reformed Church no longer opted in principle in favor of the formation of Christian organizations was resented by these groups.

Still, there was also an understanding of the synod's standpoint. One of the drafters of the document was the Amsterdam professor Gerrit Cornelis van Niftrik (1904-1972), himself a prominent member of the Christian Historical Union.[1] In 1951 he had already defended the synodical policy powerfully (so principally supported what would be written later in the 1955 document). His defense came in a sensational speech on the occasion of a conflict in Hardegarijp[2] between the proponents and opponents of the establishment of a new Christian school.

The Reformed Church council of Hardegarijp feared that the proposed new school would lead to a division in the congregation, and so it had declared itself opposed to the plans. The synodical agency in matters of education had supported the church council in its stand. Van Niftrik, speaking at a gathering of the National Body of Reformed Teachers, explained why the Reformed Church did not opt unambiguously for Christian education and against public education.[3] For the church it is always, so he said, about the youth of the entire nation.

The Apostolate in Practice: The Synod and Politics

Thus the Reformed Church, through the policy of its synod, took seriously the principle contained in its church order, that it understood itself to be called to the apostolate and that this included engagement in and for the society as such. It explicitly did not leave such engagement to particular societal or political groups or parties formed by Christians. It wanted to be more than an advocate of interests or the mouthpiece of a particular sector of the population, and, consequently, it did not want to resign itself to the notion of the neutral state. In its public declarations it continued to address government and population from out of "God's promises and commands" (as it was stated in the church order).

---

[1]   A political party of that era.
[2]   A township in the province of Friesland.
[3]   That is, education offered on behalf of the state.

Over the years, many writings came from the synod that had to do with a variety of contemporary political and societal subjects. These publications were often attacked heavily from political circles (not the least of which were the Christian-Democratic). The synod was for the most part advised by its Council for Governmental and Societal Affairs in this matter, a gathering of experts from relevant areas.

One of the subjects was the colonial question. The policy of the Dutch government, which was focused on maintaining colonial power in Indonesia, was questioned with growing criticism. The most critical came from the Reformed synod in 1956 (advised by the Council for Mission), in its "Call to Reflection" in the matter of New Guinea: "The Netherlands must be prepared to drop its claim to govern New Guinea solely on its own authority."

Another controversial issue was the question of war and peace. The Reformed synod issued ever more urgent declarations of its conviction of the fatal nature of the nuclear weapons race. In the report, *The question of nuclear weapons*, issued in 1962, it was stated that use of these weapons is not to be justified by any goal; in any case Christians

> cannot responsibly, before their consciences, bound as they are to the Word and promises of God, offer their cooperation to a war with nuclear weapons.

A "radical no" was expressed against the use of nuclear weapons, even in the case where the "enemy" would begin a war from his side with the use of nuclear weapons. And a plea was advanced for steps to be taken (provisionally one-sided if need be) to break through the mutual mistrust that ruled between East and West.

Further developments in the weapons race were the occasion for a pastoral letter in 1980. The standpoint of 1962 was sharpened in this letter; not only the use, but also the possession (and threat) of nuclear weapons was also branded as unacceptable. The massive peace demonstrations of the 1980s were organized by the Interchurch Peace Council, which was established in 1966 in part by the Reformed Church.

Still another matter that required thought was the policy of apartheid in white South Africa. Above all, the fact that the policy of apartheid was supported by Christian arguments, derived from the Bible, and put forward by the white *Nederduitse Gereformeerde Kerk*[4]

---

4   "Dutch Reformed Church." The Dutch East Indian Company established a

compelled the synod to an ever more critical position. This criticism was also directed at the Dutch government and Dutch businesses. In the judgment of the synod (which was ever more explicitly informed by the black churches in South Africa), Dutch government and business put too little pressure on the South African regime. They were, for example, not prepared to promote disinvestment.

When discussion with the businesses involved (conducted together with other churches) brought no change, the Reformed synod in 1986 called its own agencies to withdraw from businesses investing in South Africa if they had invested funds in their portfolios at their disposal. Some of these bodies (bearing their own financial responsibility) heeded the call. Others, however, judged disinvestment not to be necessary and not in the interest of the soundness of their peculiar ecclesiastical financial positions. In these matters, some of the—often-vehement—discussions were echoed within the church as well. Meanwhile, the policy of apartheid in South Africa was officially abolished in 1994, and the matter is no longer current.

A fourth political/societal subject on which the Reformed synod expressed itself publicly was the unification of Europe. This topic became current after the Communist government collapsed in Eastern Europe in 1989, thus bringing a definitive end to the cold war between East and West. In 1991, the Reformed synod published a *handreiking*[5] on the necessity for a common assimilation of the history of the cold war for the churches in both East and West. In 1996, the report, *Heart and Soul for Europe?* followed. That report addressed developments that have been underway since 1951 in the movement toward the European Union.

In this report, the synod expressed its support for the European struggle for integration on the basis of the original intention behind it—the promotion of reconciliation, peace and justice. It maintained that European unification may not be limited to Western Europe. The churches (often promoters of nationalism in the new, post-cold war situation) should and must assist this unification to their utmost capabilities. Witness to the gospel of Jesus Christ in Europe is, furthermore, not the same as striving for the restoration of a "Christian Europe," so the synod stated.

settlement on the Cape of Good Hope in 1652. Its purpose was to provide provisions for the ships of the company. The settlement included the establishment of a Reformed congregation.

5   "Helping hand" or "guidelines for reflection."

The examples given above are but a small selection. The Reformed synod has expressed itself over still other societal questions. They include, among others, social-economic policy and poverty, global and national; the peaceful application of nuclear energy; pollution and the use of the environment; such medical-ethical questions as artificial insemination, euthanasia, and abortion; and marriage and sexuality. It has always, faithful to its apostolic vocation, been willing to address both government and populace as well as its own church members according to "God's promises and commands" with an eye on the quality of the society.

In growing measure, the synod acted as it did together with other churches in the context of the Council of Churches of the Netherlands (newly established, in part by the Reformed Church, in 1968). Here the actions and pronouncements were less and less specifically Reformed initiatives. The Reformed Church was indeed one of the driving forces of common interchurch/ecumenical actions in the society, as had also been the case during the Second World War (with the then-existing Interchurch Consultation).

Foundations and Perspectives of Confessing

Besides the apostolate, thought was given to confessing.[6] Here, too, a course was set forth that had been prepared in the war and afterwards was sanctioned by the church order. The intent was to strive for a new confessing of faith, on the basis of new biblical insights and in the face of contemporary questions. People hoped for a confession that could be commonly supported in the church, with all the division among its parties.

Already in 1949, the synod accepted the document, *Foundations and Perspectives of Confessing*, as a (temporary) "draft" of what was intended.[7] This writing was drafted entirely in the form of a complete confessional document. The entire Christian faith is set out here in nineteen articles.

The central thought and the beginning point is the confession of "God, our king," whose lordship ("kingdom"/"kingship"), however

---

6   The Dutch term is *belijden*, which is a verb, in contradistinction from *belijdenis*, which is the noun and would represent a more permanent product. The synod is stating clearly that confession is an act, something the church does that cannot be petrified in a document. A confessional church, then, would be a confessing church.

7   Translated into English as *Foundations and Perspectives of Confession* (New Brunswick, N.J.: New Brunswick Theological Seminary, 1955).

much contested and denied by human, has prevailed in Israel and in Jesus Christ and will continue to prevail.

As in the document, *We Believe and Confess,* dating from 1943, the significance of Jesus Christ emerges from a discussion of the various aspects of his work—prophetic, priestly, and royal. Therewith it was hoped to transcend the traditional opposition between left and right over the question whether Jesus is "also God," or (exclusively) "true human."

Noteworthy are the closing articles on the actions of God in the (contemporary, ongoing) history, on the "presence and future of Israel," and on the "completion." Here insights were advance that had not previously appeared in classic Reformed confessional writings. In the passages concerning the current significance of the Jewish people ("Israel"), we hear echoes of the experiences of the war.

In the article on "the government," we find the principal foundation of the apostolic attitude of the Reformed synod, described above, in the face of government and society. That article speaks of a "particular place" that God has given "in his plan of salvation" to those who rule. In order to be able to fulfill their (ordering, protecting) calling, "those who rule must continually seek God's commandment for our society." Rulers may "not be neutral...but must...seek to represent the Kingship of God and to praise Jesus Christ as the highest of the kings of the earth."

Government and church, so it was said, serve together in God's plan, but not in the same way: "The church preaches God's salvation. The government orders the outward life in accord with this salvation." The government is bound to listen to the preaching of the church, but has a peculiar "independent responsibility to God."

Foundations and Perspectives was drafted by a commission consisting of representatives of all parties within the Reformed Church. Among others, professors Miskotte and Van Ruler participated. The principal drafter was Berkhof. He had also written a detailed explication (as he had done with *We believe and confess*).

The document was discussed in gatherings of the classes following acceptance by the synod. Fairly critical reactions came, above all from circles of liberal Reformed and (for opposite reasons) from the *Gereformeerde Bond. Foundations and Perspectives* was not accepted as an official, new confessional writing of the Reformed Church. Yet, the writing did stimulate much reflection on the issue of "confessing."

New Reflection on the Doctrine of Election

That reflection went further in the context of the synod as well. Again and again, discussions within the church as well as new trends in theology pressed the synod to occupy itself with specific questions of faith, with the intention of guiding the thinking of church members.

One of the questions concerned the doctrine of election. We have seen that sharp discussions were conducted on this matter already in the seventeenth century. The Canons were accepted by the synod in 1619 on this matter (in the controversy with the Remonstrants), and since then have been considered an official confessional writing of the Reformed Church.

We learned how in that document the emphasis was laid on the powerful initiative of God who "from eternity" has "elected" some to salvation, in distinction from (many) others. We also heard how later many Reformed orthodox in the Reformed Church (the Further Reformation and the *Gereformeerde Bond*) have clung powerfully to just this conception. Among these groups, the Canons of Dort were and are still viewed as an indispensable keystone of the entire building of Christian truth.

However, for many others the doctrine presented in this issue was anything but evangelical and comforting. They heard in the doctrine a logical, unbiblical, unmerciful determinism that gives short shrift to human responsibility. For still others, the question of election as discussed in the Canons of Dort played scarcely a role in their experience of faith. Thus, on just this point, the different parties in the Reformed Church have often stood squarely opposed to—or are at least distant from—each other.

The confessional writings do not have an unshakably valid authority anymore. The new church order has officially opened the possibility to introduce a gravamen.[8] It must, of course, be defended by an appeal to the Bible.

A minister from Ziest, A. Duetz, made use of this possibility in relation to the Canons in 1953. His gravamen presented the synod with an occasion to install a broad-based study commission. In 1960 the commission's report was accepted by the synod and published as a "guideline for the handling of the doctrine of election."

[8]   Or a "grievance" often allowed in Reformed church orders. A gravamen that is introduced requires a higher assembly to take cognizance of a complaint, usually against a matter of doctrine.

With great respect for the Canons of Dort, the report nonetheless states that the argument of the Canons follows a Western, logical way of thinking that does not do justice to the biblical message in all its aspects. The question, "Am I among the elect?" is not present in the Bible. And, again in the Bible, contrary to our logical thinking, God's actions and human responsibility are not experienced as opposites. Believing thought is simply different from theoretical thinking. Arminius and the Remonstrants were at least partly correct in their support of human responsibility and the universality of God's grace, although they too remained imprisoned in a logical-theoretical scheme of thought.

With its "guidelines," the synod hoped to be able to contribute to a new, positive relation between the Reformed Church and the Remonstrant Brotherhood. That indeed did happen, although it has not led to a reunion.

Discussion of Maintenance of Confession and Doctrinal Discipline

Other questions of faith on which the synod expressed itself (largely advised by its Council on Church and Theology) included the authority of the Bible (how it is, and is not, to be understood), atonement

> (has Jesus died for our sins? And how must that be understood?), future expectation for the dead, the question of what the church (congregation) really is, and the meaning of the Lord's Supper (can and may children also participate? And if so, under what conditions?).

The commissions charged to work on these matters were over and over again constituted to be as broadly based as possible, to include members with backgrounds in the various parties in the church. Yet, during these years, the work of the commissions often succeeded in reaching a final decision that was accepted by a clear majority of the synod. In so doing, the church continued to cling to the very notion that originated during the war years, the consciousness of being the church together over and against party differences.

The oppositions certainly continued, albeit less sharply than previously. They emerged specifically in discussions on the question how one had to deal with the maintenance of the confession. In the church order of 1951 (differently than in the earlier *Algemeen Reglement*), the possibility was officially included that—in extreme cases, following a careful procedure—doctrinal discipline would be practiced. Ministers and church professors who in their preaching and teaching oppose the Bible and break with the "communion with the confession of the fathers" could in extreme circumstances be removed from their offices or functions.

The official introduction of this possibility was a radical break with the condition that had existed since 1816. Liberals viewed such prescriptions in the church order with horror. In contrast, orthodox members, specifically from the circles of the *Gereformeerde Bond*, had long urged the active maintenance of the confession, including the use of doctrinal discipline.

Meanwhile, the synod took a careful course. With the acceptance and the introduction of the new church order in 1951, "transitional prescriptions" were enacted as well. Among others, they included the statement that the articles having to do with the possibility of the removal of a minister from office after ascertaining that he contradicted the confession would not become effective for ten years. It was deemed that this delay was necessary to give the church the chance to orient itself to its new responsibility in its "oversight of the ministry of the Word."

In 1961, the ten-year period came to an end. In that year the synod published the pastoral document, *On the Confession of the Church and Its Maintenance*, as an aid for responsible action. In it was emphasized on the one hand that the possibility of doctrinal discipline is necessary; not everything is allowable in the Christian church. On the other hand, the far-reaching and thus precarious nature of the exercise of doctrinal discipline was pointed out. It means more than stating that a particular doctrine (notion of the faith) cannot be tolerated in one's own church. It means, rather, that a doctrine may not be tolerated in any particular church because it does not belong in the entire church of Christ. To say that sort of thing, you must, of course, be certain of your business!

For yet another reason, warning was brought against a too-fierce passion for doctrinal discipline. There is the danger that one too quickly curtails innovations without having asked sufficiently whether new insights might not be responsible to Scripture. There must be room in the church for thought experiments.

Moreover, one must not think that doctrinal discipline should be the most important task of the church, as if a church is a confessing church only when it practices doctrinal discipline. No, the act of confessing happens in many ways—in preaching, in praise, in the Sunday church service, even, possibly, in the formulation of a new confessional writing. At its deepest, it depends on God's Spirit whether the confession obtains in the church. Humans and ecclesiastical institutions certainly bear their own responsibility. But "doctrinal discipline is an extreme means which must be practiced as little as possible."

These considerations were much too cautious for the orthodox in the Reformed Church. The liberals valued them just at this point but found that the pastoral document was not careful enough. It was pointed out that procedures for doctrinal discipline would find little understanding in the climate of modern times, and thus would give a bad impression of the Reformed Church in the society at large. Doubt was expressed whether the Reformed Church in its current condition was either authorized or capable to practice doctrinal discipline. It would have to come into greater conformity with the image of the true Church of Christ. Until that stage would have been reached, it would be better for the prescriptions for doctrinal discipline in the church order to continue without force even after 1961.

Women in Office

A question that led to heavy discussion within the church was that of "the woman in office." With the reception of the new church order in 1951, the offices of minister, elder, and deacon still remained reserved to males. Proposals to allow women to be considered for election to office stumbled over resistance from broad circles in the church in 1954. In 1958, the matter was again on the agenda. It was then decided to open the offices of elder and deacon to women; the office of minister was also opened to women in exceptional circumstances. In 1966 the way for women to be called as ministers was completely opened.

Opponents of this decision appealed not only to tradition but to particular biblical texts in which the right to speak within the congregation was denied to women. Proponents also wanted to obey the Bible, but therewith they distinguished the intentions of biblical prescriptions from their time-bound form.

In the discussion, the vision of the office also played a role. Many proponents of women in office laid the emphasis on the democratic character of ecclesiastical office within a Protestant understanding. They saw the office as nothing other than the particularization of the "priesthood of believers" as that is fulfilled by all congregational members, males and females. Others saw the office more as a matter of authority over and against the congregation, standing in Christ's name. This view was advanced by some as an argument against the opening of the office to women.

The decision of 1966 did not mean the end of differences of opinion. Party differences came to light anew over this issue. To this day, the *Gereformeerde Bond* opposes women in office on principle. In its practice, however, it accepts the fact that there are women office-bearers elsewhere in the church. One does not avoid meeting such women office-bearers where one participates together in ecclesiastical assemblies. But one continues to reject as unbiblical the settled decision to open the office to women.

Differences in opinion concerning the understanding of ecclesiastical office continue to exist, despite the work of various study commissions. These differences do not follow party lines.

The 'Middle Orthodox' Synod Policy

The official course of the Reformed Church continued with the goal of transcending party differences. That course was determined by that part of the church that no longer counted itself as belonging to a particular party (liberal, confessional, *Gereformeerde Bond*).

Paradoxically enough, one spoke in this connection of "middle orthodoxy" (a term coined by Berkhof). Saying little in itself, it is a collective term for all those who knew themselves firstly to be members of the Reformed Church as such and (often inspired by the theology of Karl Barth) remained committed to the building up of the church along the lines of the new church order.

The earlier "ethical" party no longer existed. The Confessional Union still existed, but saw its essential task completed in the acceptance of the new church order and viewed its separate existence less important than its contribution to the church as a whole. In fact, the ethicals and the confessionals together became the middle orthodoxy.

A variety of attempts tried to bring the parties (so far as they still existed) into conversation with each other. In 1956, the synod published a special "helping hand" with such a conversation as its aim. The document was prepared by a broad commission, consisting of representatives from all parties. It argued, among other things, that division over ideas need not hamper the unity of faith. Instead of the term "parties," the preference in official usage was for the term "modalities"—differing ways of belief and articulation of the faith that could enrich the partners in mutual conversation.

The establishment of the theological seminary, as early as 1950 (meanwhile on the estate at Hyde Park at Doorn), was of great importance in this context. It is an institution for the practical, social, and cultural completion of the university's academic ministerial education.[9] That approach too was something new. Berkhof was the first rector in 1950. Thus he received a key position in the education of ministers.

At the seminary, again and again, students from all the faculties of theology at different universities and from the entire breadth of the church were brought together to live in residence for a few months. An intensive mutual "conversation of the parties" was pursued by the students during these months. This was a deliberate attempt to prepare prospective Reformed ministers to function together in the whole church.

The publications policy of the church was also intended to bring cohesion. Another new initiative, already in 1945, was the publication of its own weekly paper, *De Hervormde Kerk*,[10] intended as a paper for all Reformed members. In 1958, it was rechristened *Hervormd Nederland*,[11] thereby indicating that it sought readers in all the Netherlands, non-Reformed included. Also the fortnightly *Woord en Dienst*[12] was started in 1952, intended as a paper to equip all Reformed office-bearers. Here too, a broadening of its original goal occurred later, as the paper became an "organ for Reformed congregational life." Both papers wanted emphatically to distinguish themselves from the various party periodicals that continued to exist.

The goal of *Reformed Netherlands* has certainly not been realized. It has never really become the paper of all Reformed members. Declining circulation finally brought about a paper that stood on its own. For some time it has appeared under the more neutral name, *HN Magazine* (in which the letters "HN" were still a hidden indication of its origin). In 2002, its separate publication came to an end.

---

[9]   It will be helpful for American readers to understand that a university degree provides the basic educational degree necessary for ordination. The "seminary" is not equivalent to American seminaries as post-baccalaureate degree-granting institutions. In this case, the seminary adds practical education required for ministers to be admitted to ordination.

[10]   *The Reformed Church.*

[11]   *Reformed Netherlands.*

[12]   *Word and Service.*

Woord en Dienst has not achieved what it intended either. It has never really been the paper for all Reformed office-bearers. Even so, it continued into the 1990s as the official organ of the Netherlands Reformed Church.

Party Differences at the Grass Roots

In the meantime, party differences continued to manifest themselves in local congregations. In a number of places, the existing separate "gospel gatherings," liberal or orthodox, were integrated into the "official" Reformed congregation. But congregations remained where such integration did not succeed. In still other places, new gospel gatherings originated that embodied party differences. Sometimes they were established by orthodox groups within and over against an orthodox congregation because the official congregation was seen as not orthodox enough.

The leadership of the synod, of course, had to take account of this phenomenon. Efforts to draw separate groups into the framework of the church were attempted. That happened through a number of transitional prescriptions that had been appended to the church order. These prescriptions gave the executive committee (board) of the provincial synod the authority, when the need was apparent (and there was sufficient liberality) among a number of congregational members, to make emergency provisions for church services and a pastorate alongside the "official" congregation without the agreement of the local church council. The provincial synod functioned as the responsible church council for that group of congregational members and saw to the calling of a minister.

Originally, this possibility was limited strictly to specified periods of time. But such emergency provisions appeared quickly to become more permanent than the synod had intended. In 1985, the relevant prescriptions in the transitional regulations became normal, fixed regulations of the church order. There was no more talk of "emergency provisions," but of a "partial congregation." That signaled the official recognition of the painful fact that party differences still stand in the way of the communion of faith in specific situations.

About 1970: Intensified Polarization

In the tumultuous years around 1970, an intensified polarization emerged. On the one hand there was a wave of democratization that included the Reformed Church. This phenomenon induced the synod to organize a General Church Gathering (an initiative against which the *Gereformeerde Bond* signaled its principled resistance). This General Church Gathering took place in 1970 and 1971, prepared by a number of local and regional consultations. Many congregational members participated. A powerful plea emerged for a more generous recognition of the maturity of congregational members; for room for pluriformity in confessing; for less formality in church order prescriptions in matters concerning church membership; for a nonanxious ecumenicity despite ecclesiastical differences. The synod certainly had empathy for this urge toward maturity, although it could not go along with every concrete proposal.

There was during this time, in theology, also a strong accent on the call to the renewal of society. This new theology—also called "God-is-dead theology" or "theology of revolution" or "liberation theology"—was characterized disapprovingly as "horizontalism." In it one saw the consequences of the apostolate as a course advocated by the synod since the war. On the other hand, proponents of the new theology called their opponents, equally disapprovingly, "verticalists." This mutual labeling did not help mutual relations.

The opponents of the new theological thought expressed their alarm in a number of open letters, which caused a great deal of unrest. That was clearly the case with the *Witness*, published in 1971 and signed by leading ministers and theologians from confessional circles and from those in the *Gereformeerde Bond*. They saw in the (then) modern (and popular) theology a degeneration of the gospel to a purely worldly messianism and an identification of the faith with a particular (leftist) societal and political involvement. As the foundational fault of modern theology, it was pointed out that a notion of the holiness of God no longer existed. The writers advocated elements that in their opinion had been disregarded in recent theological developments: love for God's self, personal belief, salvation coming from above, from God.

In the discussions about "horizontalism" and "verticalism," people often talked past each other. To be fair, revolutionary and liberation theologians did not want to deny the holiness and the uniqueness of God. And their alarmed opponents did not want to deny that the Christian faith embodies a new way of life and the acceptance of shared responsibility for society and culture.

In November 1971, the synod dedicated a session to a full discussion of the issues flagged by *Witness*. In the declaration accepted at the close of the session, gratitude was expressed for *Witness* and a promise was given to send a "message of encouragement and enlightenment" to the congregations. However, that message did not happen. The synod could not agree on a proposed text. The proposal was nevertheless subsequently sent to the church as discussion material.

The fierce polarization on the occasion of the "new theology" died down after a few years. But party differences remained.

CHAPTER 10

After 1970, *Samen Op Weg*: From the Netherlands Reformed Church to the Protestant Church in the Netherlands

About 1970, the post-war developments came to a turning point. In the previous chapter we saw how an intensified polarization presented itself at that time. The enthusiasm of the period of rebuilding was past. The great expectations that emerged after the war had only partly been fulfilled. Secularization and "unchurching"[1] apparently had not been stemmed. In the church a new trend appeared, less lofty, more businesslike, more sober.

A New Approach to Church Finances

In chapter 7, we saw how the percentage of Reformed in the Dutch population declined between 1900 and 1930 from 48.4 to 34.5, and the percentage of those who did not belong to any church increased in the same period from 2.3 to 14.4. These developments have continued since the Second World War. In chapter 1, we already noted how the pace of those trends hastened after 1960. On January 1, 1998, the Netherlands Reformed Church included about 2.1 million members, or about only 13 percent of the population (which in the meantime had grown to nearly 16 million people), according to the church's own statistics. Sixty-three percent of the population viewed themselves as outside the church. The Netherlands is secularized.

It is no wonder that the financial position of the church weakened over time. The financial relation between church and state had long

[1]   *Ontkerkelijking.*

been maintained as it had been prescribed in 1815. The government still stood as guarantee for the payment of its portion of the salaries and pensions of Reformed ministers, together with those of leaders of the churches, "denominations,"[2] that had also, since 1815, existed alongside the Reformed Church. That governmental share remained literally the same as in 1815, with no adjustment for inflation. As a percentage, the financial assistance from the state to ministers' salaries had thus lessened enormously. Congregations had come to live under ever heavier financial burdens.

In 1983, the old financial relation between church and state (or better, what still remained of it) ended. After long negotiations between the government and church bodies, all parties agreed on a commonly accepted final payment. The state paid all the church bodies together a one-time payment of 250 million guilders, and with that the government's financial duties toward church bodies were definitively discharged. In the Reformed Church, the money received was used to increase the support of ministers' pensions, which had been under-supported.

However, it had become clear much earlier than 1983 in the Reformed Church that financial support for church work would have to be arranged differently. In the church order of 1951, the new figure of the "elder-churchwarden" had been introduced.[3] The intention (not immediately realized everywhere) was that the financial matters of the congregation would henceforth be entrusted to elders with a special task; they would thus, as elders, be members of the church council. This arrangement made it clear that financial management in the church is no less a spiritual matter than, for example, the pastorate or preaching.

That vision was the foundation for a new initiative enacted in 1971. In January 1972, a house-to-house financial action took place under the name, Church Balance, which included as many congregations as desired to cooperate. This door-to-door approach took place everywhere in the nation during the same two weeks of

---

2   "Denomination" is, of course, a notion borrowed from a North American context. The Dutch term used to adopt this concept, *gezindheid*, denotes those of similar disposition.

3   Previously, the financial management of the affairs of Dutch Reformed congregations was under the auspices of "church-wardens," most of whom were not elders or deacons. Thus, financial administration was not a responsibility of the church council.

the year. It was supported by publicity via radio and television. The idea behind the action was that request for financial support of the church was not about begging or charity, but rather about an appeal to church members to express their shared financial responsibility for the congregation. The result was surprising, not only financially (a growth of the total amount in pledged contribution per participating congregation of an average of 30 percent) but also psychologically.

In 1973, Church Balance became a common national program of seven churches (which include, besides the Netherlands Reformed Church, the Roman Catholic Church and the Reformed Churches in the Netherlands). The driving force was the Rotterdam minister Willem Hendrik den Ouden (b. 1919). This shared program has been repeated every year up to the present. Many volunteers participate in the work.

The total amount pledged yearly to the congregations for contributions has continued to show growth (although it is no longer as spectacular as in the first years). And that while the number of members who contribute declines year after year. It has been ever fewer members of the congregations who together contribute ever more to the church.

The End of Euphoria: Displeasure with the National Church

But the financial burdens on the churches continue to increase as well, and they do so at a faster pace. That makes it increasingly difficult to fund the work of the general synod and its many agencies of assistance. The money for that work must continually flow from the congregations to the national church. It is understandable that in less wealthy congregations, displeasure emerged at the high amount of the required payment. The question began to be heard louder and louder whether reductions could not and should not be made at the national level.

Displeasure over the national church had existed for a longer time, particularly, as we have seen, with the *Gereformeerde Bond*. Critical voices from others united with them during the 1980s, including those from the circle of middle orthodoxy. The euphoria over the church order of 1951 was past. People criticized its formalism, its unwieldiness (as the General Church Gatherings of 1970 and 1971 had done), a structure of ecclesiastical offices that was too heavy, and the overbearing pretension that the church can and must always act in societal matters. A new, less cumbersome church order had to emerge so that the church could become (in the words of Groningen professor Gijsbert D. J. Dingemans, b. 1931), "a house to live in."[4]

Congregational Existence in the Global Society

This new trend worked its way through the synod. To be sure, the course of the apostolate, established after the war and ratified in the church order of 1951, was not abandoned. In 1988, the synod published a "pastoral assistance" booklet, *Congregational Existence in the Global Society*. The wording of the title expressed the intention that the booklet be linked with the synod's document of 1955, *Christian Existence in the Society of the Netherlands*. But the difference in the title was a clear signal of a shift in orientation. While the central thought in the 1955 document concerned the role of the national church in society, the thought in the 1988 document focused more on the congregation, the church in its small connection, the local configuration of the existence of the church. At the same time the thought given to Dutch society was expanded to include worldwide society. The existence of the church on a small scale as presupposed and argued here signifies no narrowing of vision. It is coupled with a global orientation.

In its new document, the synod intended to take secularization into account. Pillarization,[5] with its accompanying idea of antitheses, which had so thoroughly captured thought (and that compelled opposition in 1955), was past. From the perspective of society at large, the church had become a marginal phenomenon. It was no more than one group, with its world view, alongside many others. This situation had not been foreseen in 1955.

This state of affairs is valued positively in *Congregational Existence in the Global Society*. The church (congregation) is put on its own feet. It is thrown back on its own reason to exist. It can no longer comfortably rely on a "Christian" culture. That is healthy. On the other hand, however the document did not deny that the "historic relation between Christendom and western culture" still remains in effect and that it has particular advantages: "It is still possible to address western society about the values that have partly been derived from Christendom."

As noted above, the document identifies the tendency toward globalization alongside the trend toward secularization. The world has

---

4   The title of a book by Dingemans, *Een huis om in te wonen*, published in 1987.
5   See p. 72, note 8.

come close. Each congregation, however small or local, is itself directly related to the global society. This relationship is not something extra; it touches the heart of congregational existence itself. The effect is that the congregation believes differently, and confesses differently.

Above all, the global relationship means being confronted with the need and the suffering that are worldwide. It is this confrontation that challenges the congregations anew to confess and to witness. That confrontation is about articulating "who Jesus Christ is for us today, in light of the wounded places in global society and in light of human suffering." "Lines of conflict that have to do with the most basic questions of humanity" transverse our world. A sharper view of these fault lines can "draw us closer to Christ." For it is no less true that we meet Christ in the poor and the oppressed than that we meet him in Christian worship around Word and sacrament.

It is also in this engagement with and through the victims that the ecumene originates as a worldwide network of communication from congregation to congregation.

The national church is not left out of the picture in *Congregational Existence in the Global Society*, but it stands in the background. The trans-local church structure, so it is said, "stands in service of congregational existence." That must also be considered in reflection on the significance of synodical statements. Today, such statements no longer have the more or less self-evident authority that they still had earlier within and outside the circle of church members. When the synod speaks or publishes, it does so—when it is done well—in service to and rooted in consultation with the congregation. If that is not the case, it remains but a lofty pronouncement. If its reflections do connect locally, it can and will engage the questions of the day. The authority of such expression depends on its content; those outside the church look for certified expertise, those in congregations look for recognizable biblical content.

Such considerations are not new in themselves, but they are certainly being advanced with greater emphasis than previously. What it means to be called as a church to the apostolate has become a point of discussion. Also, various reports from the executive committee gave the synod repeated opportunities to reflect on this matter since 1988. It has issued statements with contemporary questions at the foreground less often than in the first decade following the Second World War. It deems itself no longer called to this task as often. And it is no longer the right time to issue such statements.

Samen op Weg[6]: **The Beginning**

Meanwhile, the Netherlands Reformed Church, together with the Reformed Churches in the Netherlands and the Evangelical Lutheran Church in the Kingdom of the Netherlands, became engaged in a process of church unification. The renewal of the Reformed Church in and after the Second World War had already prepared the way for contacts between Reformed and *Gereformeerden*. With the introduction of the new church order in 1951, the Reformed Church had again officially become a confessing church. Could, and should, the church divisions of the nineteenth century not be reversed?

The real driving force came from below: from eighteen ministers (nine Reformed and nine *Gereformeerden*), all active in missionary work. During a gathering held at Church and World April 24, 1961, they decided spontaneously to publish an appeal. In it, they claimed "that the division of the Netherlands Reformed Church and the Reformed Churches of the Netherlands can no longer be borne" and that there "must be a striving toward unity." They said that they made this appeal "moved by the expectation of the kingdom of God and the task of the church in the world." The Reformed could recognize this as the same apostolic motive that had provided the impetus to the postwar renewal of their own church.

The challenge of "the Eighteen," published on Pentecost 1961, found a great response. Thousands took part in national and regional gatherings, which were subsequently held in 1962 and 1963.

Those involved in youth work in the Reformed and *Gereformeerde* churches took up the torch. They presented a joint report to the 1969 Reformed and *Gereformeerde* synods in which they urged that the synods themselves should embrace the matter of church reunion. The synods listened to this urging. That was the official beginning of the reunion process that henceforth would derive its name from the title of that youth report: *Samen op Weg*.

The Reformed and *Gereformeerde* synods gathered in a common assembly for the first time in 1973. Henceforth, such common sessions took place once every three years, from 1982 every other year. Confessional questions were discussed, as well as church order prescriptions that were necessary to make shared work possible, sketches for future shape of the intended common church. Shared ministries indeed had their origin in a number of local situations.

6   "Together on the way."

Sometimes it went so far that the Reformed and *Gereformeerden* became practically one congregation, with one shared minister.

1986: 'In a State of Reunion'

In 1986, the synods declared that both churches lived "in a state of reunion." By that was meant that unity has certainly still not been reached, but the process of unification was no longer a condition in which the participating churches could remain aloof; the process was irreversible.

This joint declaration was based on a document accepted at this same common synod, a *Declaration of Agreement on a shared ecclesiastical existence*. In a number of central points, it registered how much the Netherlands Reformed Church and the Reformed Churches in the Netherlands agreed in confession. In addition, a number of outstanding differences between the two churches were identified. However, these differences did not form, so it was claimed, an occasion "to continue our divided ecclesiastical existence." Indeed, there was every reason to reflect on the questions together.

The points of difference at issue in essence concerned two questions, both of which have to do with the vision of what the church is. The first question concerned the boundaries of the church. Who is within and who is without? As for the Netherlands Reformed position one could consider "birth members," a membership category unknown to the Reformed Churches in the Netherlands. Who belongs as a "member," and who doesn't?

The second question had to do with the relation of the church to the government and the populace. Does the church as national church bear a special responsibility toward the society? Or is that responsibility born only by church members, by Christians personally? As for the Netherlands Reformed position, one could consider the post-war radical rejection of the Christian formation of groups (pillarization) as a principle, one highly honored on the other hand, in the Reformed Churches of the Netherlands, following in the footsteps of Kuyper.

It was on the basis of these considerations that in 1986 the declaration concerning the "state of reunion" could emerge. In that same year, the small Evangelical Lutheran Church joined the *Samen op Weg* process. Henceforth this process is no longer headed for church reunion, but for church union (the Lutheran Church has always been a separate church group). Since 1990 the common assembly of the synods has been an assembly of three synods.

Concretely on the Way to a United Church

Likewise, the participating churches agreed in 1990 on the route that had to be traveled actually to achieve unity. A common work group was established and charged with the task of preparing a new church order for the one church of the future. In due time, this church order could replace the separate church orders of the three churches. Then they would be in a position to make the definitive decision to become one.

The proposed church order was presented already in 1992. The text was determined in provisional form and sent on to all classical assemblies and all church councils in the three churches. They answered with a flood of reactions and proposals for amendments.

In 1995, the accompanying new procedures (*ordinanties*) for the enactment of the church order were placed on the table as a proposal. They were drawn up in a provisional version by the three synods in 1997. There too, church councils and classical assemblies reacted with a mountain of commentaries.

In these years common synod assemblies were no longer an exception. They had to be held many times each year, and, as time went on, they replaced the regular, particular assemblies of the separate synods.

In the meantime work toward the melding of the different agencies of the three churches was undertaken with great energy and with the help of professional organizational advisers. This work progressed extremely quickly. In 1994, the publication of a common official paper, *Kerkinformatie*, began; the publication has since appeared monthly. In 1998, all previously existing separate Reformed, *Gereformeerde*, and Lutheran councils and commissions along with their accompanying staff, were ended. In their place emerged a new, shared structure, led by a general director.

All national activities were concentrated in the National Service Center established in the former Military Hospital in Utrecht. The beautifully renovated building opened December 1, 1999, with Queen Beatrix present.

Netherlands Reformed Objections to *Samen op Weg*

The process of unification of the churches themselves, however, did not proceed so quickly. It was primarily in the Netherlands Reformed Church that increasingly vocal objections were voiced as this process moved ahead. It was particularly the *Gereformeerde Bond*, with its conspicuous spokesperson Jan van der Graaf (b. 1937) as general secretary, which was very vocal and visible. In less measure, the Confessional Union was also upset.

From the outset the *Gereformeerde Bond* left no doubt that it had insurmountable objections to the course of this process. The objections were concentrated more and more on the proposed church order that included the principal outlines of the future united church.

The *Bond* dedicates itself, without conceding any ground, to recognizing the authority of the classic Reformed confessional writings. That struggle had already compelled the *Bond* to take a critical stance over and against the post-war policy of the Reformed synod and the church order of 1951. However, in the *Samen op Weg* process, the *Bond* saw the authority of the Reformed confessional writings threatened much more seriously.

The *Bond*'s reservations had primarily to do with the fact that Lutherans were involved along with Reformed and *Gereformeerden*. The Lutheran Church had its own confessional tradition. The Lutheran confessional writings are assuredly very closely related to the Reformed, but there are differences. Thus, the Lutheran confessional writings do not include a doctrine of election as do the Canons of Dort.

This last matter is not an unimportant detail for the *Gereformeerde Bond*. The *Bond* views election as the summation and the confirmation of Christian doctrine. Whoever attacks this point of faith, so claims the *Bond*, neglects God's sovereignty on which in the end all depends— whether or not a human being finds grace.

In Article I of the church order of the united church, the Lutheran and Reformed confessional writings are set next to each other, and it is stated that the united church is "bound" to the Lutheran as well as to the Reformed tradition. Moreover, the *Concord of Leuenberg* is cited. That document is a declaration of agreement drafted jointly in a European context by Lutherans and Reformed. The old differences between the two traditions are viewed as no longer current. And a few critical remarks are made concerning the classic Reformed doctrine of election.

The fact that the *Concord of Leuenberg* is named explicitly in the new church order is a thorn in the eye for the *Bond*. It saw the document's inclusion as an even stronger indication that the Reformed confession would no longer enjoy untrammeled authority in the future united church.

The *Gereformeerde Bond* had yet a second serious objection to *Samen op Weg*. That had to do with its vision that the Netherlands Reformed Church (its official name since 1816) was the legitimate continuation (despite all its faults) of the Reformed Church in the Republic of the United Netherlands, and thus from its early history tightly bound with the nation of the Netherlands and its history. The *Bond* lives in the conviction that this church is the one established, truly "planted," by God among the Dutch people in the sixteenth century.

It is for that reason that the *Gereformeerde Bond*, however much it sympathized with the zeal for the confession of Kuyper and his followers, still did not share in the *Doleantie*. The *Doleantie* was, finally, a human work, not God's work. Humans simply cannot begin a new church on their own initiative. Well now, wasn't the *Samen op Weg* process also human work, and in the same manner? Here another human construction was erected that attempted to replace the church directly planted by God in the Netherlands.

This idea also existed outside the circles of the *Gereformeerde Bond*. It came to expression in the *Hervormd Pleidooi*[7] as an open letter addressed to "the assemblies and members of the Netherlands Reformed Church." It was published in March 1994 and signed by twenty-one Reformed (mostly ministers and theologians). On this issue, confessionals and a single liberal Reformed Church member found themselves alongside members of the *Gereformeerde Bond*.

However, the *Gereformeerde Bond* represented this position as an organization. It deemed it unacceptable that the Netherlands Reformed Church would be lost (and so disappear) in a "church" constructed anew. That the proposed church order (in Article II) presented the new united church as "the continuation" of the Netherlands Reformed Church (as of the Reformed Churches and the Evangelical Lutheran Church as well) could not deflect the *Bond* from this objection; fanciful words in the church order could not cover up the fact that it was still about the disappearance, because dissolution, of the Reformed Church.

This objection cohered with the fact that an agreement could not be reached easily on the name that the united church would carry. At first, in 1993, it had indeed agreed on the name: "United Protestant Church in the Netherlands." The word "Protestant," of course, was a compromise, acceptable to Reformed, *gereformeerden*, and Lutherans, although it was not anyone's first choice. But later objections arose

---

[7]   "Reformed plea."

from the Reformed side against the fact that the word "Reformed" did not resonate in the name.

Again, these objections did not come only from the *Gereformeerde Bond*. Others, primarily confessionals, shared them as well, or at least were of the opinion that to guard against a division in the Reformed Church one must meet the desires of the *Bond*. These objections achieved a majority in the Reformed synod in its assembly of March 1998. There it opted for the name "United Reformed Church." However, this name was unacceptable to the Lutherans. However fully agreement was reached over the entire text of the proposed church order, a definitive confirmation had thus far broken down on the question of the name.

Going Away or Going Along?
The *Gereformeerde Bond* Divided Internally

For a long time it remained uncertain what attitude the *Gereformeerde Bond* would take when the church union intended by the *Samen op Weg* process actually came about. In November 1992, at an extraordinary, well-attended gathering of office-bearers organized by the board of the *Gereformeerde Bond*, the pithy rallying cry was raised: "We cannot go along and we cannot go away."

To the ears of outsiders, this rallying cry sounded internally contradictory. For would one by not "going along" in church union not in fact "go away"? And vice versa, would one by not "going away" not in fact "go along" with church union? For the *Bond* itself, however, the rallying cry expressed precisely the dilemma in which they saw themselves caught. People expected to be able to hold out in this dilemma because they refused to accept that church union would really happen.

Yet after a few years it became evident that one had to choose between "going away" and "going along." At another extraordinary gathering of office-bearers, in September 1996, the *Bond* opted for "going along." The *Bond* would remain at its post in the united church under protest. In that connection it would then continue to stand for the authority of the Reformed confessional writings as it has always done within the Netherlands Reformed Church. And it committed itself to the cause of including provisions in the church order that would allow for the possibility of congregations of a Reformed tradition (thus *Gereformeerde Bond* congregations), within the united church, to continue their own ecclesiastical life, albeit mutually connected on a trans-local level. The Reformed synod from its side, together with the two other synods, sought painstakingly to meet this desire.

The policy chosen by the board of the *Gereformeerde Bond* cited above led to a split within the membership of the *Bond*. Some of its members took the very opposite choice in the dilemma articulated above; they chose to "go away." They formed a separate organization, the "Committee to maintain the Netherlands Reformed Church," a small but extremely contentious group. Office-bearers and congregations that belong to it declared that they, in the case of a church union intended in *Samen op Weg*, would continue themselves as the "true" continuation of the Netherlands Reformed Church.

Church Unification Achieved:
The 'Protestant Church in the Netherlands'

Despite all the resistance to *Samen op Weg*, the unification process neared its goal. In a special meeting of the combined synods, held in April 2002, the synod board unexpectedly announced its plan to aim for a final decision on unification to be taken in December 2003. It had concluded that the discussion of the objections and the efforts to satisfy the opponents within the context of the unification plan could not continue indefinitely without doing harm to the entire church.

This announcement provoked intense activity within the church on all sides. Once again fierce opposition appeared. At the conclusive discussion on the church order, those articles that would allow local church councils to open the possibility for alternative (that included homosexual) relationships to be "blessed" in the worship services of the local community provoked a great deal of commotion. In June 2002, after a long and emotional debate, the synod rejected all protests and adopted this new regulation. Of course, no congregation would be forced to accept this possibility for itself against its will. But that was no comfort to those opposed.

At the same synod, a formal proposal, submitted jointly by the *Gereformeerde Bond* and the Confessional Union, to refrain from formal unification and instead to work toward a "federation" of the three churches (which would thus maintain their independent existence alongside each other) was discussed. In this proposal, in fact a repetition of what had been proposed on earlier occasions, fundamental opposition to unification as such was combined with the pastoral concern: would not another church split be the consequence of unification? The synod, however, was of the opinion that federation was not a real option. It rejected the proposal for federation and persisted in unification as the matter on which a decision would have to be taken.

Despite continuing opposition, a decision was reached on the text of the new church order in the summer of 2003. At that time a majority decision could also be reached on the name of the future church—"Protestant Church in the Netherlands"—almost identical with the name that had been rejected in 1998. The only difference is that the new name no longer speaks of the "United Protestant Church." Does not the word "united" contain a silent reference to a continued existing plurality? Is it not superfluous when one speaks of a (one) "church"? For the Netherlands Reformed Church, the qualification "in the Netherlands" is a useful reminder that the church is not and cannot be a (Dutch) national church. The notion that the church and nations could coincide is rejected by implication, not only as unreal, but as a misunderstanding.

When the text of the new church order had been agreed upon, the decision on church unification remained to be taken. For that, a special meeting was held in Utrecht December 12, 2003. It had been agreed earlier that for this important decision to be valid, a two-thirds majority would be required. It was to be a narrow escape: in the end, of the seventy-five members of the synod of the Netherlands Reformed Church, twenty-four voted against unification. If only two more members had opposed the union, the unification would not have taken place so far as the Netherlands Reformed Church was concerned.

On the same day, the national synods of the *Gereformeerde Kerken* and the Evangelical-Lutheran Church held their decisive meetings on the same issue, again in Utrecht. In those meetings, the opposition was far weaker than it was in the Reformed synod. At the end of the afternoon, it was noted with relief that all three synods had agreed to unification. That evening, a common evening prayer was held in the Dom Church, the ancient cathedral in the center of the city. Queen Beatrix and representatives of the Dutch government were present. It was a joyful gathering, although the joy was dimmed in awareness of the continuing opposition.

By May 1, 2004, the Protestant Church in the Netherlands had officially become a fact. The three separate synods had completed their respective mandates. A new synod, representing and leading the Protestant Church, had been elected and had already met for the first time March 12. In the meantime, a split could not be avoided. History is repeating itself. Despite all efforts to keep the opponents on board (through the work of special pastoral committees and through the possibility offered by the synod board that congregations could specifically identify themselves as "Reformed congregations" "attached to the Reformed confessions alone"), sixty-eight (of the some fourteen hundred) congregations declared themselves unwilling to participate in the new Protestant Church and intending to continue their own existence as "Reformed" congregations independently.

By May they had created a separate ecclesiastical community with the provisional name, "Re-established Netherlands Reformed Church" (*Hersteld Nederlandse Hervormde Kerk*). According to the authorities of the Protestant Church, however, the use of this name is considered illegal because it unjustly gives the impression that the Protestant Church is not itself the continuation of the Netherlands Reformed Church. If no agreement can be achieved, the matter will be brought to court. In some local communities, bitter conflicts arose between those ministers and members who desired and those who did not desire to become part of the Protestant Church. To ministers, to be outside the Protestant church will mean loss of their legal status and right to income. It appears as though they are fully willing to accept this consequence. Sadly, in some cases, efforts to prevent people from continuing on their path to separation seem to be in vain.

The Congregation as Central in the Future United Church

A few more words are in order on the character of the Protestant Church as it exists and as it currently is developing. First, we look once more at the National Service Center, the church's main office, located in Utrecht. Its establishment, in 1999, was already a down payment on the one church that was to come.

The name, "National Service Center," was consciously chosen. It stated explicitly that the church intended to place the priority on the local congregation, the church at ground level. It is intended that the national office function as an instigator of activities in the congregations. A more modest purpose is expressed. Services are offered of which the congregations themselves have need. Moreover, activities (primarily missionary, diaconal, ecumenical) are performed which the congregations cannot do separately; that too means service to the congregations.

With this attitude one meets the criticisms leveled against the "supra-local apparatus" which could be heard specifically in the Reformed Church in the last decades. The entire conglomeration of councils, commissions and offices, as it had grown since 1945, was considered too expensive, and furthermore as superfluous. All sorts of work was done that was not wanted in many local congregations, to the extent that they were aware of all these activities. In this appraisal, a criticism was also voiced that concerned the synod itself. The synod had functioned too often in a pioneering role in the post-war years, or so it was thought.

We have already heard how, apart from *Samen op Weg*, displeasure over the functioning of the synod had grown in the last decades of the twentieth century in broad circles in the Reformed Church. Different insights had emerged in the synod itself in the 1980s, insights by which more emphasis was laid on the local congregation as the central configuration of the nature of the church.

In the *Samen op Weg* process the same trend was at work. The leading thought behind the establishment of the National Service Center, which appears already in its name, is but one indication of this fact. One can see this trend as well in the new church order. It begins, of course, with a number of articles on "the church" (the existence of the church in a national context), after which follow articles on "the congregation," the existence of the church locally. Then in the large second main section that handles the various aspects of ecclesiastical life and work, however, the congregation stands at the forefront. The heart of the church beats in the congregation; the proposed church order lays the emphasis on the congregation more than the Reformed church order of 1951 did.

The fact that the term, "apostolate," does not appear in the new church order points in the same direction; it was precisely that word that stood so very central in the post-war Reformed church order. Of course, not everything depends on the words one uses. In the new church order apostolic notions certainly appear. For example, it states (in Article I-6): "The church witnesses God's promises and commands before humans, powers, and authorities."

But what was added to this phrase in the Reformed church order, namely, that the witness "to government and people" is intended to direct "life in conformity to God's promises and commands" remains absent in the new church order. That is not as unimportant a detail as it appears.

The new church order speaks much more modestly of the missionary calling of the church than did the Reformed church order of 1951. The emphatic sequence of the Reformed church order—first the "apostolate" of the church and thereafter the confession—is not to be found in the new church order. In fact, the apostolic nature of the church is here seen as implied *within* its confessional nature. Thus it is not accidental that the term, "apostolate," is missing in the proposed church order. The apostolic nature of the church is no longer central in the new church order. What stands central in this order is the particular life of the (local) congregation.

A synod that expresses itself on current social and political questions fits well in a church order where the apostolate is placed at the center. A church order that places the life of the congregation at center and that above all else intends to be modest about the church's apostolate is suited to a synod that keeps to the background and seeks less publicity.

One could have expected the development of the *Samen op Weg* process to follow a different path. Its first initiative—the appeal of "the Eighteen"—emerged from an apostolic passion. The "Declaration of Agreement on the common existence of the church" had the same apostolic motif sounding through it. The Reformed and the *Gereformeerde* drafters brought the appeal to the (then still) two churches involved "to unite our strength and to seek together a common witness of faith and life in the society of the people of the present."

In contrast, the spiritual climate today has changed dramatically. The apostolic motif is no longer the central motive behind the intended "being the church together." All is now directed to the living congregation, local, small-scale.

A New Trend: The Evangelical Workgroup

In 1995, a new group of Reformed and *Gereformeerde* ministers stepped into public view with the publication of an "Evangelical Manifesto." The group called itself the "Evangelical Workgroup."

Its goal was spiritual renewal. It expressed anxiety about the spiritual lukewarmness in the churches. "It fizzles and sparkles not often in our church." A pervasive lack of spirituality is pointed out, that is to say, the absence of a "personal relationship with the Lord Jesus Christ."

It comes down to precisely the personal relationship. It is to that that the members of the Evangelical Workgroup will dedicate themselves. With their emphasis on rebirth (personal renewal of life) and on the work of the Holy Spirit, they understand themselves to be connected with the Pentecostal movement that emerged in the twentieth century.

In this sense the Evangelical Workgroup labors for the formation of the congregations. Among other things, that includes space for what the Manifesto calls "conversion baptism (through immersion), which can be desired by adults" in addition to infant baptism. The group also published a separate evangelical songbook for use in church services (and elsewhere) besides the official songbook. That a living congregation is an attractive congregation, and thus a missionary congregation, is considered to be self-evident.

How large the number of supporters is among Reformed and *Gereformeerden* for this new trend is difficult to ascertain. It certainly represents, even in its more measured forms, a growing mentality that desires to break with the fashionable way of talking about the "crumbling ailing church" and that wants to make a positive attempt. At the same time it confirms for its part the tendency that we sketched: the direction toward the existence of the congregation in its small-scale context.

The Church of the Twenty-first Century

This tendency responds to the spirit of the age. The contemporary mature human is less willing than in former years to rely on powerful leaders and leading institutions. In a secularized and multicultural society human beings, Christians included, seek their own way, where possible together. In any case, the (united) church of the twenty-first century will look different from the Reformed Church of the twentieth century.

CHAPTER 11

The Identity of the Netherlands Reformed Church

In the preceding chapters we took a sweeping view of the history of the Netherlands Reformed Church. We have seen that the existence of that church as a separate entity has come to an end. It has now, together with the Reformed Churches in the Netherlands and the Evangelical-Lutheran Church, become part of the Protestant Church in the Netherlands, a new church body. And yet that new church is the continuation (in a new form) of what had existed previously. For that reason, we may say that the Netherlands Reformed Church survives in this new context. It is still useful, then, in this final chapter to identify the characteristics, the peculiar identity of that church.

The average Reformed Church member doesn't exist. Within the Reformed Church a great diversity has always been present among the parties, ideas, and trends. The faith conviction of one Reformed Church member is decidedly not that of another. Sometimes one gets the impression that one member stands in direct opposition to the other. We already saw that the preaching and the spiritual climate in one Reformed congregation can be miles apart from another. This is so much the case that one may ask whether there is anything that holds all Reformed people (now members of the Protestant Church) together. Nevertheless, there are some things can be identified. To a lesser or greater extent, there are particular matters which touch all the Reformed people, matters in which they are able to recognize each other, or at least understand each other, despite all their diversity. In the following discussion, I will attempt to articulate such themes. A picture of the diversity within the community of those who came into the Protestant Church as members of the Reformed Church will emerge naturally as part of that effort.

Rooted in the Reformed Tradition

The roots of the Reformed Church are embedded in the Reformed tradition as it took form in the sixteenth century, primarily through Calvin. The central thoughts of the tradition are summarized in the three classic Reformed confessional writings that since 1619 have continued to be officially authoritative: the Dutch Confession of Faith (1561), the Canons of Dort (1619), and the Heidelberg Catechism (1563). Of these three it has been primarily the Heidelberg Catechism (formulated in a question and answer format to aid in education) that has won both reputation and influence in wide circles. That impact is to be credited to the practical-pastoral tone of this document. One hears that tone immediately at the outset (Question and Answer 1):

> Question: "What is your only comfort in life and in death?"
>
> Answer: "That I, in body and in soul, in life and in death, do not belong to myself, but am the property of my faithful Savior Jesus Christ. He has perfectly paid for all my sins with his precious blood and saved me from the lordship of the devil. He watches over me with such care that without the will of my heavenly Father, no hair can fall from my head, yes, even that all things must work to my salvation. Thus he assures me also through his Holy Spirit of eternal life and makes me prepared with all my heart henceforth to live for him."

Here faith is described as having found in Jesus (and in Jesus alone) comfort and certainty for living and dying, for time and eternity, a comfort that also exists in the notion of being safe under God's fatherly care.

It is to be noted that what is said here concerns "being the property of Jesus Christ." Jesus is thus not only "my Savior," but also "my Lord," although that word is not used. I belong to him, says the catechetical student. That means that I am also called, yes even am "prepared with all my heart to live for him." This accent on the conduct of life in God's service, to the Lord's honor, is typical of the Reformed tradition.

It is equally typical that this conduct of life is seen not as a condition to be fulfilled by the human or as a demand to achieve a goal in order to receive the comfort, but as a (self-evident) consequence of the comfort received.

Faith

The opening question and answer sets the tone. What follows in the catechism is really only an unfolding of this beginning. What follows is divided into three chapters. It speaks sequentially of "how great my sins and miseries are," "how I am saved from all my sins and miseries," and "how I must be thankful to God for such a salvation" (Answer 2).

The section on the "misery" of the human creature precedes the others. It puts into the mouth of the catechetical student the phrase, "I am by nature inclined to hate God and my neighbor." The question whether we humans "(are) then so corrupt that we are wholly and completely incapable of any good and inclined to all evil?" is answered in the affirmative, but with a restriction, "unless we are born again by the Spirit of God." That restriction grants that the situation is thus not altogether hopeless. Yet at the same time it states that the hope for a better prospect must come from elsewhere, from the Spirit.

This section on "sin and misery" admittedly comes first, but it is far and away the shortest of the three. The very short first section really presents only the background for what follows. It describes why the human needs the comfort of the gospel (which is not stated in so many words but merely presupposed in the first question and answer cited above). It is all about comfort. This is broadly expounded in the second chapter, on salvation.

From the outset, salvation is demonstrated and attested to with an appeal to "the holy gospel" (the biblical message) that (and how) Jesus Christ is our Savior. As Mediator (God and human in one person), he has made satisfaction for all our sins by taking our place; thus we are therefore counted as justified before God "only on the ground of Christ's merit." That is to say, when we assent to that justification in faith. In conjunction, it is also stated that faith in essence is: saying yes to what Christ has done "for us," "for me," and accepting that forgiveness, the status of being "justified" before God, is really "also given to me."

The content of the faith is unfolded subsequently by means of a classic ecumenical text, the Apostles' Creed, the twelve "articles of faith." This confession of faith is, of course, not specifically Reformed. All churches and traditions share it in common. However, the way in which the articles of faith are interpreted in the catechism is surely specific. That happens by letting the reader hear again and again the comfort of the gospel ("I am the property of Christ; he has made perfect satisfaction for all my sins; I am safe under God's fatherly care").

Time and again, the reader, the catechetical student, may ask him or herself what "use" it is at each point to believe what is held out as an article of faith (for example, concerning God the Creator, Jesus' birth, his suffering and death, his resurrection and ascension), what "advantage" he enjoys thereby. What does it "mean"? It is to that question that each time an answer is explicitly given.

> As summary, we hear at the end of this part (in Question and Answer 59):
>
> Question: "What advantage is it to you now, that you believe all this?"
>
> Answer: "That I am justified in Christ before God and an heir to eternal life."

Thus, it is once more underscored that it is only through this faith that a human person receives the comfort of the gospel articulated here. And at the same time, the misunderstanding that "faith" itself is something humanly meritorious is carefully deflected. Faith is always but a hearty acceptance of what is given to you, saying "yes" to it.

The Sacraments: The 'Power of the Keys'

It is in this context that the sacraments—baptism and the Lord's Supper—are mentioned. Again it is true that this is something all Christians, all churches, acknowledge, but it receives a unique interpretation. The sacraments are presented here (in Answer 66) as "holy, visible signs and seals, instituted by God better to have us understand and to seal for us the promises of the gospel through their use."

It is about the "promises of the gospel." They must be "understood" (in their meaning for salvation); that is, it is about "believing" the promises. That "understanding" is based on the Word, on the proclamation of the gospel. The sacraments serve to "strengthen" that belief, to deepen "understanding," to make the "knowledge" of the gospel a "certain knowledge." At base, so it is argued, the Word and the sacraments stand beside each other. Baptism and the Lord's Supper are (Answer 67) intended to be taken equally with the Word (the proclamation of the gospel): "to point our faith to the offering of Jesus Christ on the cross as the only ground of our salvation."

Again, we hear an echo of the beginning of the catechism, which characterizes the gospel as the message of the "only comfort in life as in death."

Thus, the sacraments can only be received where there is true faith. Such faith is required above all at the Lord's Supper. Ecclesiastical discipline also is spoken of in this context (Question and Answers 81-85). Those who "have on account of their sins turned away from themselves and yet trust that they are forgiven for Christ's sake" are heartily welcomed at the Lord's Supper. But those "who make themselves known by their confession and life as unbelievers and godless" may not be admitted to the Lord's Supper. They are excluded, and they are thus shut out of the kingdom (salvation) of Christ until they repent.

The catechism here places the topic of the power to "bind" and to "loosen," to "remit sins" and to "impute sins," or the handling of the "keys of the kingdom of Heaven," which the New Testament says that Jesus has given to his disciples (Matt. 16:19; John 21:21-23).

The catechism nowhere talks about office-bearers, ministers, elders, deacons, or the church council. But where it speaks of the proclamation of the Word and the administration of the sacraments, the "minister of the Word" is naturally present, in the background. And the catechism naturally considers the responsibility of the church council (ministers and elders together as the leadership of those congregated) where it speaks in that context, specifically in connection with the Lord's Supper, of ecclesiastical discipline, of the power to handle the "keys of the kingdom of heaven."

Christian Life: Lived Faith, the Ten Commandments

In this last instance, in the passage on the "keys of the kingdom of heaven," we hear again an indication of the theme of Christian conduct of life that also came through in the beginning of the catechism. That theme emerges fully and particularly in the third chapter, on thankfulness.

Detailed thinking on the Christian conduct of life is of itself typical for the Reformed tradition. Typical also is the characterization of the Christian life as a life of thankfulness to God for the received salvation. It thereby states immediately that salvation can not be deemed valid before God as an earned performance. Naturally, the expression of gratitude is not worthy of merit. And still it may not, cannot, and will not be omitted. As the catechism already stated (Answer 64): "It is impossible that one who is engrafted in Christ through true faith would not bear fruits of gratitude."

The Christian conduct of life is amplified in its content by the Ten Commandments (the "Law of God," Exod. 20:1-17) and by the Lord's Prayer. It is true here as well: there appear in the catechism texts which, seen by themselves, are not peculiar to the Reformed. All churches and traditions have the Ten Commandments and the Lord's Prayer (as the "perfect prayer" that Jesus himself taught his disciples according to the gospel) in common. Again, what is specific to the Reformed tradition is only the interpretation that is given, the context in which they are placed, in the chapter on "how I must be thankful to God for such a salvation" (as described in what preceded.) Of the prayer it is even said (Answer 116) that this "is the principal part of the thankfulness that God demands of us."

Each of the Ten Commandments receives a separate interpretation, as does each of the petitions of the Lord's Prayer. The attempt is always made to penetrate to the real intention behind the formulation of the commandments. Over and again more appears to be said than one can discover on the first reading of the literal text. It is emphasized that in everything one should do God's Word. Christian life is thus lived faith.

What is said concerning the second commandment, the prohibition of images, is typical:

> You shall not make a graven image nor any figure of what is above in heaven, nor what is beneath on earth, nor what is in the water under the earth. You shall not bow yourself before them nor serve them...

What God demands here is articulated in Answer 96: "that we picture God in no way and honor God in no other way than what he has commanded in his Word." Images of mere creatures are certainly not prohibited here, so the catechism concludes, but they can in no case be the object of adoration. And on the question of whether one may have images in churches as "books for the laity," and thus as aids to illustrate biblical persons and stories for those who cannot read the Bible, the answer states (98): "No, for we must not be wiser than God, who desires to educate his Christians not by dumb images but by the living proclamation of his Word."

The preference for sobriety of church buildings that has existed in the Reformed tradition from its outset, by which all is centered on the Word, the sermon, finds its classic expression here.

Typical as well is the reflection given to the fourth commandment, the "Sabbath commandment":

> Remember the Sabbath day, that you sanctify it; six days shall you work and do all your work, but the seventh day is the Sabbath of the Lord your God; then you shall do no work...

This commandment is interpreted (Answer 103) directly as a commandment for the sanctification of Sunday. Participation in the church service is in view from the outset: "to hear God's Word, to use the Sacraments, to call upon the Lord God publicly to display Christian help to the poor."

In the Reformed tradition in the Netherlands as elsewhere, the sanctification of Sunday has received much attention and has left a deep impression on public life well into the twentieth century. It played an important role in the life of many Reformed folk. That role has still not played itself out. Or at least so one might conclude from discussions that have been held about it, as well as, for example, from the protests against the importation of the "twenty-four-hour economy" that have been raised from the ecclesiastical (in part Reformed) side.

God's Commands and the Government's Task

That God's commandments are also related to public life, that God must also be served in the public life, emerges a number of times indirectly in the interpretation of the Ten Commandments. The authorities are mentioned in connection with the third commandment:

> You shall not take the name of the Lord your God in vain.

Not only are all curses forbidden, says the catechism (Answer 99) at this point, but also "unnecessary swearing." However, the swearing of an oath with the Name of God does not fall under this prohibition (Answer 101) "when the government desires it of its subjects...thereby to confirm faithfulness and truth, and certainly to the honor of God and the salvation of the neighbor." The government also serves to promote "the honor of God and the salvation of the neighbor."

In the fifth commandment, "honor your father and your mother," the catechism (Answer 104) hears the command to obedience to all in a position of authority:

> That I...show all honor, love and faithfulness to all who are set over me and subject myself to their good teaching and discipline with proper obedience since God is pleased to rule us through them.

Does this mean unconditional subjection? It certainly sounds like it. But since it is "good" teaching that is mentioned here, it leaves open the possibility that there can also be talk of "bad" teaching and discipline. Likewise, the mention of "proper" obedience leaves open the possibility that there are situations in which obedience is not proper.

Also, the interpretation of the sixth command, "Thou shalt not kill," again refers to the government, this time explicitly. You can also kill, says the catechism (Answer 105) without the application of physical violence: with thoughts, words, gestures, in vengeance...all that is forbidden (and therewith the real positive in the commandment is given to love the neighbor as one's self). And, so it says, "the government bears...the sword to prevent killing."

Thus the task of helping maintain God's command is conferred on the government. That is the issue when governmental action is under review. It is not said here in so many words that the government may, or even must, be reminded of that responsibility when necessary (for example, when in its own struggle for power it uses "the sword" too eagerly). But that it is allowed to address the government in such cases may certainly be considered in conjunction with the matter at hand.

That God's commands have no less relation to public life (and to the government's actions) than to the life of everyone personally is from the outset one of the central ideas of the Reformed tradition. It is still a Reformed conviction today, which implies that one cannot hand over society and politics to its "own laws."

In Communion with the Confession of the Fathers: The *Ecumene*

Thus far we have examined the broad contours of the Heidelberg Catechism. As has been said before, of all the classic Reformed confessional writings, it is this writing that has won the greatest reputation and influence. And that not only in the Reformed Church; it has done so as well among the *Gereformeerden*, members of church groups in the Netherlands that also carried variations of the word "Reformed" in their names (and which, in one way or another, all stemmed from the Reformed Church).

Today, the catechism itself has receded to the background. Of course, that is not true across the board. Certain sections of the (formerly separate) Reformed Church (those of the *Gereformeerde Bond*) are still involved intensively with the catechism, in catechetical education and doctrinal services, week to week, Sunday to Sunday. But that is no longer the case elsewhere in the church. There, it appears that confession "in communion with the fathers" (as it is was put in the church order of the Netherlands Reformed Church and has been taken up in the church order of the Protestant Church) is not exactly the same as confession in "agreement" with them.

That many Reformed no longer hold to the letter of the confession is in part the consequence of ecumenical contacts with other traditions and churches in world Christianity. From the beginning of the World Council of Churches in 1948, the Netherlands Reformed Church has been a member church. In the course of the years since then a number of representatives of the Reformed Church (laity, ministers, theologians) have played a large role in the work of the World Council. One was the first secretary general of the Council, Willem Adolph Visser 't Hooft (1900-1985). From the beginning there was enthusiasm for the ecumenical movement among many Reformed people. That is still the case, although in recent years interest in the fortunes of the World Council has waned markedly.

Believing Today: Jesus the Forerunner and Path Maker

In any case, the focus of the gospel on the message of Jesus Christ as "Mediator" who has made "satisfaction" for sins "with his blood," as the Heidelberg Catechism presents it, evokes questions from many people today. That focus is often experienced as a reduction of the biblical message. Is the message not also, or even above all, about liberation from meaninglessness? Is Jesus not proclaimed in the Bible above all as the herald and onset of the "kingdom of God," God's lordship that will make all things new? Must not attention be given to his earthly life, to his preaching, his acts of healing as narrated by the gospels and not only to his suffering and death? Is the Easter message of Jesus' resurrection, however it must be understood, not a message of hope and new beginning? In the seventies, on the initiative of the Council of Churches, a multiyear project was pursued in the

Netherlands, seeking to come to a common, new articulation of what it means to confess Christ. The project was undertaken to give "account of the hope that is within us" in contemporary circumstances. Persons and groups from a variety of churches in the Netherlands were invited to begin to give such an account by putting it in writing. Many participated enthusiastically. One group, consisting of Reformed participants, drafted their own confession as follows:

> We live together
> this existence of ours
> of unwillingness and surrender
> of guilt and perspective
> because Israel's God has chosen
> for humanity and the world.
> We cannot ignore Jesus,
> his life is the turning point,
> his Easter the ground of our hope.
> To believe is to succumb to him
> to be caught up in his renewal movement
> which moves through the entire world
> in a solidarity that transcends borders.
> To hope in God is
> to dare to give up your own project,
> to move on a new course, a little at a time
> making visible something of God's mercy
> among the needs of all.
> To hope is
> to allow yourself to be called away
> from slothfulness and platitudes,
> not to be stuck in your own wisdom
> together breaking out,
> out of silence and ambiguity.
> A way out of the paralyzed feeling
> of the equivalence of good and evil,
> as living in communion
> toward and on the basis of the kingdom
> that God will establish:
> a world that is whole, with genuine human beings.
> Hope is
> hearing and putting into practice

that our choice and commitment
vulnerable and guilty on the way with each other,
matter
and persevere together.

In this new confession of faith one can discern what lives in broad circles of the Reformed Church, even though this confession is no longer all that contemporary. It dates from 1976. That was, it is true, a different time from the present. One can detect that in the text. It breathes the atmosphere of optimism and world betterment. Today, those tones have been muted considerably. Today one prefers, modestly, to speak of "right doing" and "faithfulness" as the foundational attitude of humans personally, in which the "door" for God's future is "held open." That God will have the future break forth in God's time remains the perspective for all.

In any case, today different emphases from those of the Heidelberg Catechism are to be noted in the faith experience and its articulation among many Reformed people. That is not to say that they are contradictory accents. That Jesus is seen primarily as the Man of Easter, as the one who precedes us in a new way and manner of life, does not mean the elimination of the confession that he is Savior and Mediator. The unique significance of Jesus confessed by the catechism in these terms is not altered. Indeed, the significance is only given different interpretation. Jesus is the forerunner who points the way, the path maker who opens for us the way to God's future and makes it passable. That too means "salvation," although it is understood differently than in the catechism.

That Christian faith is translated into a walk of life is stated in so many words in the catechism. This connects firmly with the contemporary faith experience of many Reformed people. Although the reading of the Ten Commandments as a regular practice in the Sunday church service has disappeared in many Reformed congregations (many of which are now, in the context of the Protestant Church, called Protestant congregations), reflection on many ethical questions, what it means to live well, continues unabated as a matter of interest for many. The Reformed share that emphasis as something they have in common, as part of the Reformed tradition, although the question of what concrete obedience to God entails is not answered by everyone in the same way.

The Centrality of the Bible

There is continuity with the faith of the catechism also in the weight that is still given to the Bible as the Word of God among Reformed people.

In the past, the question how the phrase, "the Bible as the Word of God," must be understood was discussed endlessly. Is the Bible then not a human book? Yes indeed, but the humans, the writers of the Bible, did not write on the mere basis of their own thoughts. They were "inspired" in their writing by God, by God's Spirit. The question then returned to ask how far that inspiration went. Has God, so to speak, whispered to the writers what they must write, literally?

Today, no one would make that last claim, at least no Reformed thinker. In the past centuries the Bible has become an object of intensive scientific inquiry. It has become clear that the Bible is a collection of a variety of writings, texts, and fragments from a number of time periods. The human character of the Bible is exposed more than ever before.

Still, such inquiry has not made the Bible merely an "ordinary human book." Precisely this remarkable book, the deposit of witnesses (prophets, apostles) from Israel and from Jesus' setting, continues to be experienced as peculiarly authoritative, still as "Word" from God.

For those who know something of the weighty discussions concerning interpretations and perspectives on the Bible through the centuries, it is remarkable to observe how rarely the Heidelberg Catechism engaged those discussions head-on, or at least how little the catechism gave occasion to them. The Bible, as such, is not named in the catechism. Certainly, it mentions God's "Word," God's "gospel," in which, so it is stated, God has revealed God's self, and has given us his promises and commands. That points, above all, to the living proclamation. And of course, that proclamation is unthinkable without the Bible as the source from which it draws.

It is clear in any case, that the focus is thus not about the Bible as a book in itself. It is about its content as it comes to us: comforting and admonishing and thereby authoritative. That authority is a matter of principle because it is a matter of ever new experience.

Reformed people disagree with one another over a number of points in the interpretation of the Bible. Even so, when and where the interpretation of the Bible is at stake, they find one another because they agree that it is interpretation of the Bible that is decisive for church and for life. According to an opinion poll in 1996, 98 percent of all Reformed people had Bibles in their homes, and 51 percent of the Reformed read it regularly, or at least sometimes. The retelling of the biblical stories, which an Amsterdam minister, Nico ter Linden (b. 1936), has published in book form since 1996, enjoys great popularity, not exclusively among Reformed people, but certainly among them as well.

We saw that there are great differences among the church services of the various originally Reformed (now "Protestant") congregations. This is so, for example, regarding the celebration of the Lord's Supper. While in congregations of the *Gereformeerde Bond* the number of celebrations of the Lord's Supper remains limited (the official minimum is four times per year), in other Reformed congregations the Lord's Supper is celebrated monthly or even weekly. That corresponds with a new view of its meaning; the Lord's Supper is experienced less as a pointing to and an underlining of the one offering of Jesus at on the cross, and more as a contemporary gathering with Jesus, the living, resurrected Lord. This new vision is to be found in new liturgical texts. But even so, a great accent falls on preaching and Bible reading. For the experience of many Reformed folk, it depends on how well the sermon communicates whether the service can be called a success. If the sermon, as biblical proclamation, disappoints, the celebration of the Lord's Supper does not offer a counterbalance.

Interest in the Old Testament and Judaism

The great interest in biblical interpretation also involves the Old Testament, the stories and prophecies from Israel. This interest has been present in the Reformed tradition from the beginning and has increased because of the experiences of the Second World War. The persecution of Jews not only led to protests in the Reformed Church but to new reflection as well on the continuing unique significance of Jewish people for Christian faith.

The notion that "Israel" is not only something of the past but also of the present emerged anew partly as a consequence of the establishment of the state of Israel in 1948. Judaism is very much alive and as such is a challenge for Christians. It is an impetus for a new study of the Bible, specifically of the Old Testament.

The challenge was taken up by the Reformed Church. At various times, the Reformed synod published statements and documents on the topic. There is, in the former Reformed church order, a passage concerning the "conversation with Israel"—to which the church knows that it is called—that it at least "seeks," in the hope that Israel also desires to join such a discussion from its side. In the church order of the Protestant Church, a passage now deals with the "solidarity with the people of Israel" as something that "cannot be given up" and that has to be made concrete in church life.

The notion of solidarity with the Jewish people is widespread and deeply anchored among Reformed people. Generally speaking, people have now largely distanced themselves from earlier thought (also widely spread at that time) that the church as the "people of God" would now have come "in the stead of Israel." On the question of what consequences that has for the Christian belief in Jesus as Messiah, thoughts certainly diverge. Nevertheless, people are united in the common notion of solidarity with the Jewish people.

Berkhof's *Christian Faith*, an Influential Book

The continuing unique significance of Israel for Christian faith is one of the characteristic themes in the one book that certainly can be seen as the most influential book among Reformed people in the last quarter of the twentieth century. That book is *Christian Faith*,[1] from the hand of Hendrikus Berkhof, the early rector of the seminary in Doorn, and from 1960 to 1981 professor at Leiden. This book, which first appeared in 1973, underwent a sixth, reworked, edition in 1990 (and an eighth edition in 2002, seven years after the author's death). It is still in use in many courses as a handbook for dogmatics. The vision of the Christian faith developed by Berkhof has become popular and forms for many Reformed (and for many others as well) the context of their own reflections on faith.

Berkhof takes the Bible seriously as a book of history, not just as a book of myths and profound stories. Stated more precisely, the Bible is about the history of God's covenant with people. God began with that covenant, but he has in view the human creature's response to that covenant. Israel was God's "test garden." In his involvement with this people God wanted to try out his covenant. The Old Testament relates that story. This perspective also allows one to see that God's experiment with Israel failed.

The New Testament narrates how matters went further. Jesus is, said Berkhof, "God's successive and decisive step in the continuation

[1]   Published in English as, *Christian Faith: An Introduction to the Study of the Faith* (Grand Rapids: Eerdmans, 2000).

of the way he had previously gone with Israel." Jesus, born of Israel, was what Israel was supposed to be: God's "Son," i.e., God's faithful covenant partner; the true, "completed covenantal human," given as such by God's own self. He brings the way of Israel to fulfillment. In Jesus God's covenantal intention could finally "land" in the world; now the covenant has indeed succeeded. All the while, God's faithfulness had been victorious in the midst of human unfaithfulness (represented in Israel); with Easter (Jesus' resurrection from the dead) that has become definitively clear.

From this Easter point onward, the covenant extends itself into the human world. It is now the intention that humans be engrafted into this one covenantal human and therefore are taken up with him into the covenant with God. This engrafting is the work of the Holy Spirit. In this way the "church" originated and unfolds. So too, history further develops in an ongoing process of renewal of humanity and the world. Berkhof is convinced that whoever is open to that, on the basis of faith in Jesus, can also perceive signs of that continuing process today, here and there in all its ambiguity. Ultimately all will be new, therein answering God's creational intentions.

However, the particular place of Israel in God's intentions is not, said Berkhof, abrogated with the coming of Jesus. Israel has not, by-and-large, recognized the victory of God's faithfulness in Jesus' appearance. Where the church deems that salvation has come principally with Jesus, Israel sees salvation (the Messiah) as still purely future, to be expected as the answer to the hoped for and expected human conversion to God.

For the church that is a beneficial difficulty. It is reminded by Israel that after Easter, the fullness of salvation has still not arrived. And it cannot rid itself of Israel, although it has tried to do so through the persecution of the Jews or mission to the Jews. When it writes Israel off on account of Israel's rejection of Jesus as Messiah, it writes itself off. That God's faithfulness is stronger than human unfaithfulness is valid first of all for Israel (see the Old Testament). The church as well is dependent on God's faithfulness in that way.

Thus the church continues to believe that Israel and its Messiah will some day find each other and that the signs of God's covenant are not lacking in Israel, even now. Israel as a separate people continues to be, in the present, a provisional period of salvation, related to a separate land. It remains a special address of God's faithfulness and promises. Thus the question may not be evaded whether the return of many Jews to the old "promised land," culminating in the proclamation of the

State of Israel in 1948, has something to do with the fulfillment of God's promises. The land as the dwelling place promised to Israel from of old would have to be something like a sacrament for Christians of God's faithfulness to the Jewish people.

These are the main lines of Berkhof's vision of the faith. Others would not articulate the faith in so systematic a way. It is not to be thought that Berkhof's theology is the standard theology of the Reformed Church. Such a standard theology does not exist. But Berkhof's exposition certainly includes several elements that speak to many Reformed people. I give four:

First, his understanding of the Bible as a book of history. Berkhof takes seriously (and literally!) the biblical stories as stories of what really happened (without thereby degenerating into fundamentalism and clinging to the letter of the biblical text). He provides a solid grounding for people who are Bible believers and yet want to be modern.

Second are his central theses concerning the "covenant." This has been a central idea in the Reformed tradition from the outset. It has played a particular role precisely among Reformed folk. We will return to this shortly.

In the third place is his special consideration of Israel, the Jewish people. That Jesus was a Jew, born of Israel, is essential for Berkhof. Apart from that reality the significance of Jesus cannot be well understood by Christians, according to him. Not all Reformed thinkers can find themselves in the manner by which Berkhof gives meaning to Jesus, but the accent on Jesus' relation with Israel is understood by many from the heart. It determines even more their own relationship with Israel. It should be clear that hereby faith in Jesus as the Christ is not diminished but rather more firmly anchored.

Finally, there is Berkhof's positive, ultimately optimistic view of contemporary events. That God also rules today and is active in realizing his plans is made concrete here. Thereby a hand is extended to those who want to read the Bible along with the newspaper. The biblical message evidently has to do with what goes on in the present. Fainthearted persons are given a new heart here. Christian faith appears genuinely as a matter of contemporary life and of participation in it socially and politically. Even so, this idea holds true, as a living reality from the earliest days of the Reformed tradition, quite apart from the way that Berkhof works it out.

Volkskerk and Covenant

In the above, a number of topics are named as characteristic of the Reformed Church (now a part of the Protestant Church), and of the identity of a Reformed faith, although it had also to be said time and again that they are not exclusively Reformed. The Heidelberg Catechism is an official confessional writing among *Gereformeerden* as well and among members of other church bodies that call themselves Reformed. The Reformed Church is not the only heir to the Reformed tradition. However, the manner in which a way is sought to find a path to live in "communion" with the confession of the Reformed tradition and, *at the same time, precisely thus* desires to be open to new insights, new answers of the faith that emerge from contemporary life, is typically Reformed indeed.

That search for and openness to new insights is leading Reformed people in different directions. Thus, the division within the Reformed Church has always been a characteristic phenomenon of this church. In the foregoing chapters we have seen that this characteristic definitely presents problems. That the Reformed nonetheless remain together within one church (now, together with others, within the Protestant Church) happens because people still know themselves as rooted, together, in the Reformed tradition.

One thing must still be added. Reformed people have always seen their church as involved with the people of the Netherlands and its history par excellence. We saw how the origin of the Netherlands Reformed Church was most closely connected with the origin of the independence of the Netherlands and how it consequently fulfilled the role of the national church in the Dutch system of government during a number of centuries. That position came to an end a few centuries ago. And yet something of it has continued among Reformed, albeit more for the one than for the other.

The mentality of the *volkskerk* has always lived in the Reformed Church, with its aversion to the drawing of strict boundaries between who does and who does not (any longer) belong to it. To a large extent, this mentality has been brought as a heritage into the Protestant Church. Here one still understands oneself as a church for the entire people, in service to the entire society. Today, the notion of the apostolate that was in vogue during and after the Second World War has long been forgotten. However, another notion is still very much alive among the Reformed, that of the covenant.

We saw that this word has always played an important role in the Reformed tradition. Reformed people readily hear in that word an indication of God's faithfulness that includes all people and accompanies them from generation to generation, from parents to children, in the same way that the Old Testament talks about it in relation to the people of Israel. Thus the Reformed administration concerning membership included, as we heard, not only "confessing members" and "baptized members" but "birth members" as well.

In the Protestant Church that terminology has been omitted. The new church order states that the church has only "confessing members" and "baptized members." The idea of birth membership has not totally disappeared, however. One passage in the article on church membership reads: "remembering the faithfulness of the covenant God, the congregation also considers belonging to its community the non-baptized children of congregation members."

Reformed identity is not that of a well-described, uniform faith conviction. It is more akin to a concept of solidarity, the concept of belonging together with the God of the covenant who does not leave God's self without witness in the history of the people of the Netherlands. That concept is still alive within the contemporary Protestant Church.

Index

[Names of Dutch persons are indexed by the Dutch convention. E.g., A.A. van Ruler would be listed as: Ruler, A.A. van. Americans of Dutch descent, on the other hand, are indexed according to an American convention. E.g., James W. Van Hoeven would be listed as: Van Hoeven, James A.]

159

The Historical Series
of the
Reformed Church in America
Books in print, William B. Eerdmans, publisher

This series was inaugurated by the General Synod of the Reformed Church in America acting through its Commission on History for the purpose of encouraging historical research and providing a medium wherein this knowledge may be shared both with the academic community and with the members of the denomination in order that a knowledge of the past may contribute to right action in the present.

The series was conceived in 1967 with its first volume published in 1968 with the above statement of purpose. The volumes of the series are described below in order of publication. Volumes are published in paperback in 5 1/2 x 8-inch format unless otherwise noted. All have been published by the Wm. B. Eerdmans Publishing Company under the general editorship of Donald J. Bruggink.

Herman Harmelink III
Ecumenism and the Reformed Church
Describes the ecumenical relations of the Reformed Church in America from its earliest years to 1950, including a final chapter, "Future Prospects," projecting possibilities through 1970. Pp. viii, 112, bibliography, and index. 1968. Out of print.

Elton J. Bruins
The Americanization of a Congregation
A case study tracing the Americanization of the Third Reformed Church in Holland, Michigan, from its establishment in 1867 as the second Dutch-speaking church in the colony of Albertus C. Van Raalte to its centennial celebration. Pp. vi, 122, illustrated, appendices, and index. 1970. Out of print. A second edition is available.

Dorothy F. Van Ess
Pioneers in the Arab World
Missionary biography of John and Dorothy Van Ess, beginning in Basrah, Iraq, in 1902. The account moves through the collapse of the Ottoman Empire, WWI, the intervening years and the intrigue surrounding WWII. This was an enlightened time when sheiks, mullahs, maharajahs, governors, and generals came to astute missionaries both for information, knowledge, and to act as go-betweens. Lighter contacts involved such personages as Agatha Christie. All of this was ancillary to their primary tasks of education and being a witness for the gospel. Pp. iv, 188, illustrations, bibliography. 1974. $10.

James W. Van Hoeven, editor
Piety and Patriotism, 1776-1976
Includes the following essays: _"The Reformed Church and the American Revolution," by John Beardslee III; "The American Frontier," by James W. Van Hoeven; "Immigration," by Elton J. Bruins, "World Mission," by Herman Harmelink III; "Theology," by Eugene P. Heideman; "Social Concerns," by John A. De Jong; "Education," by Norman Kansfield; and "The Role of Women in the India Mission, 1819-1880," by Barbara Fassler. Pp. vi, 191. 1976. $10.

Gerald F. DeJong
The Dutch Reformed Church in the American Colonies
From its beginnings in Europe, DeJong traces the history of the Reformed Church in America from the arrival of its first minister in 1628 through the eighteenth century. Special attention is paid to ministry, church life, relations with Indians and blacks as well as its gradual Americanization and separation from the Netherlands. Pp. viii, 179, bibliography and index. 1978. Out of print.

Peter N. Vandenberge
Historical Directory of the Reformed Church in America, 1628-1978
Superseded by the 1628-2000 volume. Pp. xx, 385, 6 x 9". 1978. Out of print.

Mildred W. Schuppert
A Digest and Index of the Minutes of the General Synod of the Reformed Church in America, 1958-1977
Contains a digest of the actions of the highest deliberative and legislative body of the Reformed Church as well as the names of all those directly involved in General Synod actions. In all cases there are references to the complete actions of the synods as found in their annual minutes. Pp. xxii, 120, 6 x 9". 1979. $11.

Mildred W. Schuppert
A Digest and Index of the Minutes of the General Synod of the Reformed Church in America, 1906-1957
The same content as above, but covering the prior fifty-one years._ Invaluable reference works regarding the interests and actions of the church during the respective time frames. Pp. xviii, 286, 6 x 9 ". 1982. $20.

Gerald F. DeJong
From Strength to Strength: A History of Northwestern, 1882-1982
This Northwestern was founded by the Reformed Church in America in Orange City, Iowa, on the American frontier. Its ethnic and religious setting, together with its development from pioneer school to academy to junior college to fully accredited four-year college is told by historian DeJong, a former Northwestern professor. Pp. x, 213, illustrations, index. 1982. $15.

D. Ivan Dykstra
B. D., A Biography of my Father, the Late Reverend B. D. Dykstra
Legendary professor of philosophy at Hope College for many decades, Dykstra

writes a fascinating biography of a brilliant, eccentric father, Yale student, minister, linguist, writer, editor, bookseller, and pacifist. B. D. was born in the Netherlands and nurtured on the northwest Iowa frontier. The book also offers insight into the Dutch immigrant community. Pp. vi, 153. 1983. $10.

Cornelia Dalenberg with David DeGroot
Sharifa
The biography of a missionary nurse, born to farm parents in South Holland, Illinois. Dalenberg served in Bahrain with the famous Dr. Paul Harrison, beginning in 1921. Her other fields of service included a leper colony in Amarah, visits to Basrah, WWII, continued service in Bahrain, medical "touring" in Arabia, and visits to Qatar. Pp. xviii, 233, illustrations. 1983. Out of print.

John W. Beardslee III, editor
Vision from the Hill, Selections from the Works of Faculty and Alumni, published on the Bicentennial of New Brunswick Theological Seminary
The Hill refers to the location of the seminary; the vision is that of many of its illustrious professors and alumni. Excerpts from the works of Livingston, Cannon, McClelland, Berg, Talmage, DeWitt, Schenck, Taylor, Worcester, Zwemer, Beardslee, Muste, MacLean, and Sizoo are included. Pp. xii, 157. 1984. $10.

Howard G. Hageman
Two Centuries Plus: The Story of New Brunswick Seminary
The account of this first institution devoted solely to the clergy is followed from its single professor in the person of John Henry Livingston through its development, its adversities and triumphs. Because Hageman was at the time president of New Brunswick, he felt it only proper that someone else should describe the contemporary scene. Chapter 13 by Benjamin Alicea. Pp. viii, 215, illustrations. 1984. $15.

Marvin D. Hoff
Structures for Mission
Describes the gradual development within the polity of the Reformed Church in America of structures that enabled the church to become a leader in international and national mission. The account moves from 1628 to 1980 and includes charts of mission boards and agencies, as well as a chronology. The role of fundraising is included as well as organization. Pp. xxvii, 243, bibliography. 1985. $15.

James I. Cook, editor
The Church Speaks, Papers of the Commission on Theology, Reformed Church in America, 1959-1984
The papers include "The Historical Character of the Book of Genesis"; "Revised Declaration on Holy Scripture"; "A Confession of Faith"; "Notes on the Doctrinal Standards as they Relate to the Scriptures"; "The Place of the Standards in the Life of the Church"; "The Baptism of the Holy Spirit";

"The Fullness of the Spirit"; "Authority and Conscience in the Church"; "A Statement on Infant Baptism"; "Infant Dedication an Alternative to Infant Baptism? "; "Baptized Non-Communicants and the Celebration of the Lord's Supper (1977 and again in 1984) "; "Concerning Rebaptism"; "The Nature of the Ministry"; The Nature of Ecclesiastical Office and Ministry"; "The Evangelistic and Social Task of the Church"; "A Reformed Theology of Nature in a Crowded World"; "Christian Observance of the Lord's Day"; "A Critique of the Thought of Sun Myung Moon"; "Christian Faith and the Nuclear Arms Race"; "A Biblical Perspective on the Conversion of the Jews . . . "; "The Holocaust and Christian Witness"; "Some Guidelines for Officiating at Marriages"; "Biblical Perspectives on Marriage, Divorce and Remarriage"; "Abortion"; "Moral and Spiritual Values Raised by the Practice of Abortion"; "Maleness and Femaleness"; "Homosexuality: A Biblical and Theological Appraisal"; "Christian Pastoral Care for the Homosexual." Each section bears an introduction by the editor placing the study in its context. Pp. xviii, 268. 1985. $20.

James W. Van Hoeven, editor
Word and World: Reformed Theology in America
The contributions include "Orthodoxy and Piety: _Two Styles of Faith in the Colonial Period," by John W. Beardslee III; "Dort and Albany: _Reformed Theology Engages a New Culture," by James W. Van Hoeven; "New York and Holland: Reformed Theology and the Second Dutch Immigration," by Elton M. Eenigenburg; "Saints and Sinners: Secession and the Christian Reformed Church," by M. Eugene Osterhaven; "Immigration and Authority: the Reformed Church Engages Modernity," by Paul R. Fries; "Prose and Poetry: Reformed Scholarship and Confessional Renewal," by I. John Hesselink; "Heidelberg and Grand Rapids: Reformed Theology and the Mission of the Church," by Eugene P. Heideman; "Piety and Patriotism: Reformed Theology and Civil Religion," by Dennis N. Voskuil. Pp. xxiii, 166, index. 1986. $15.

Gerrit J. tenZythoff
Sources of Secession: The Netherlands Hervormde Kerk on the Eve of the Dutch Immigration to the Midwest
The origin of this volume was a doctoral thesis done under Martin E. Marty at the University of Chicago. Accordingly, the study is detailed and objective in analyzing the social, political, and religious contexts leading to the secession from the Netherlands Hervormde Kerk and emigration to America. Pp. xxii, 189, index. 1987. $15.

Gordon J. Van Wylen
Vision for a Christian College
A collection of essays and addresses given by the president of Hope College, Gordon J. Van Wylen, between 1972 and 1987. The introduction was written by Harry J. Boonstra and Elton J. Bruins. Pp. xxx, 220. 1988. $15.

Jack D. Klunder and Russell L. Gasero, editors
Servant Gladly: Essays in Honor of John W. Beardslee III
"Recollections of the Beardslee Family," by Marion de Velder; "Advocacy

for Social Justice in the Reformed Church in America," by Arie R. Brouwer; "Reformed Perspectives on War and Peace," by John Hubers; "A History of Synodical Opposition to the Heresy of Apartheid: 1952-1982," by Jack D. Klunder; "The Origins of the Theological Library at New Brunswick," by Russell L. Gasero; "From Calvin to Van Raalte: The Rise and Development of the Reformed Tradition in the Netherlands, 1560-1900," by Elton J. Bruins; "From Pessimism to Optimism: Francis Turretin and Charles Hodge on 'The Last Things,'" by Earl Wm. Kennedy; and a bibliography of works by John W. Beardslee III. Pp. xviii, 134, index. 1989. $12.

Jeanette Boersma with David DeGroot
Grace in the Gulf, the Autobiography of Jeanette Boersma, Missionary Nurse in Iraq and the Sultanate of Oman.
Beginning her ministry before the end of WWII, Boersma passed through Baghdad to Basrah, where after two years she was sent to Amarah and later to Oman until her retirement in 1986. The index enables one to find her interaction with other personnel of the Arabian mission. 1991. Pp. xix, 296, illustrations, index. $20.

Arie R. Brouwer
Ecumenical Testimony
Divided into three sections. "For the Healing of the Nations" recounts Brouwer's involvement in social action and justice issues, from working with the Russian Orthodox in the nuclear days of the Cold War to addressing apartheid in South Africa and racial and justice issues in the States. "For the Unity of the Church" deals with ecumenical issues on the local, national (NCCC), and international levels (WCC), in all of which Brouwer was intimately involved. "For the Renewal of the Tradition" reveals his commitment specifically to the Reformed Church in matters of worship, education, and relations with the Christian Reformed Church. Pp. xx, 329, illustrations, index. 1991. $20.

Daniel J. Meeter
Meeting Each Other in Doctrine, Liturgy, & Government
An account of the history of the Constitution of the Reformed Church in America, which comprises its doctrinal commitments as expressed in the creeds and the Reformed confessions, together with its liturgy and *Book of Church Order*. This solid historical study speaks to immediate concerns of our identity as a church, and as such is essential reading for all who are in positions of authority and leadership within the church. Pp. xi, 212, indices. 1993. $15.

Gerald F. De Jong
The Reformed Church in China, 1842-1951
Beginning with an overview of the political context in which mission took place within the period, De Jong traces the efforts of the Reformed Church in America from its first missionary, David Abeel, to the expulsion of American

missionaries as the United States entered the Korean War. Sensitive to the cultural context, the missionaries hastened to train indigenous leadership. They also offered a Romanized script so that common people could become literate. In their determination to create one indigenous church in common with Presbyterians and the London Mission they offered to resign rather than organize a separate denomination. By the fourth decade of the twentieth century women were included in ordained church offices. Pp. xiii, 385, illustrations, index. 1992. $28.

Russell L. Gasero
Historical Directory of the Reformed Church in America, 1628-1992
Superseded by the 1628-2000 volume. Pp. xv, 440, 6 x 9". 1992. $40.

Allan J. Janssen
Gathered at Albany, A History of a Classis
Set thoroughly within its historical context, the book traces the development of this unit of church governance (roughly equivalent to a Presbytery) from 1771 and its beginnings with a new nation, through its reaching into Canada, its response to the revivalist movement from 1820-50, its growth and outreach, the development of its rights and responsibilities, its mid-twentieth-century activism, and a case study on the ordination of women. Pp. xi, 163. 1995. $12.

Elton J. Bruins
The Americanization of a Congregation, second edition
The volume (see above) has been brought forward in time and furnished with twenty-two appendices, including the names of church members in church vocations, elders, and deacons and their dates of service. Appendices are also devoted to superintendents of Sunday schools, presidents of Ladies' Aid, Women's Missionary Society, Women's Missionary Auxiliary, Reformed Church Women's Ministries, church organists and choir directors, members serving the board of Holland's public schools, charter members, and ordained and installed ministers and their years of service. The index includes the names of everyone included in the book. Few churches have been graced with such a scholarly and comprehensive history. 1995. Pp. xxiii, 235, illustrations, index. $15.

Gregg A. Mast
In Remembrance and Hope, the Ministry and Vision of Howard G. Hageman
This scholarly tribute to one of the great leaders of the Reformed Church in the twentieth century is divided into thematic sections: "Our Worship," in pulpit, at table, in prayer and praise; "Our Work" in ministry; "Our Witness" in South Africa and in our cities; and Howard's stellar lectures, "A History of the Liturgy of the RCA." Included is a chronology of the life and work of Hageman, including sermons, lectures, and publications. Pp. xxiii, 229, illustrations, appendix, index. 1998. $18.

Janny Venema, translator & editor
Deacons' Accounts, 1652-1674, First Dutch Reformed Church of Beverwijck/Albany
The deacons of the First Church of what is now Albany kept meticulous

records of both income and distributions of their funds. These resources, sometimes in beaver pelts, sewant, or currency, were collected both in church and in alms boxes in taverns. Expenditures were for food for the poor, rental of a pall for funerals, repairs to homes of the indigent, for nails, and "for one half barrel and one anker of small beer used by Clas Ullenspegelt when his wife was in childbed" (p. 39). An invaluable insight into seventeenth-century Dutch colonial life. Pp. xxi, 293, glossary, bibliography, index, 6 x 9". 1998. $30.

Morrell F. Swart
The Call of Africa, The Reformed Church in America Mission in the Sub-Sahara, 1948-1998
Missionary biography and autobiography of Robert and Morrell Swart beginning with their service in the last days of the Anglo-Egyptian Sudan, then in the independent Sudan; their removal to Ethiopia when civil war broke out; and yet a third period of mission in Kenya. The mission in the Sudan took place primarily in Akobo and Pibor, in Ethiopia in Omo, and later in Alale, Zambia, Nairobi, and Malawi. Told with vivacity and intimate personal insight into mission life. Pp. xvi, 536, illustrations, maps, glossary, index. 1998. $35.

Lewis R. Scudder III
The Arabian Mission's Story: In Search of Abraham's Other Son
A scholarly history of the Arabian mission of the Reformed Church in America by a missionary to the Mideast, born of missionary parents who served that mission. Scudder presents a background of Middle Eastern mission, a history of the development of the Arab nations, and a history of the missions of the Reformed Church. The main areas of mission in education, evangelism, and medical work are chronicled, together with the areas of mission in Basrah, Bahrain, Kuwait, and Oman. Also included is a history and analysis of the varying relationship of the mission to the denomination and home churches. A magisterial history. Appendices include a timeline of the Arabian mission and missionary appointments and distribution by station. Pp. xxvii, 578, bibliography, index, 6 x 9". 1998. $39.

Renée S. House and John W. Coakley, editors
Patterns and Portraits, Women in the History of the Reformed Church in America
Joyce D. Goodfriend writes of women in the Colonial Dutch Reformed Church; Johan van de Bank exams the piety of Dina van den Bergh; John W. Beardslee III describes Dutch women in Two Cultures; Firth Haring Fabend describes the evangelical mother in Reformed Dutch households in nineteenth century New York and New Jersey; Elton J. Bruins and Karsten T. Ruhmohr-Voskiul tell the Christina de Moen Van Raalte story; Russell Gasero describes the rise of the Woman's Board of Foreign Missions; while Renée S. House analyses the work of the *Mission Gleaner*. The preparation of women for foreign missionary service is described by Jennifer Mary Reece, while Joyce Borgman de Velder shares her memories of the struggle for the ordination of women. Carol W. Hageman describes the decline, fall and rise of women in the Reformed Church, 1947-1997; and Mary L. Kansfield writes of New Brunswick Theological Seminary women past and present. Pp. xiii, 182, index. 1999. $15.

Elton J. Bruins and Robert P. Swierenga
Family Quarrels in the Dutch Reformed Churches of the Nineteenth Century
The account begins where the tenZythoff (cf. above) volume ends. From the *Afscheiding* of 1834 through immigration, union with the Reformed Church in America, the secession of 1857, and a mass secession in 1882, the story is briefly but objectively told. Pp. xviii, 158, illustrations, bibliographic essay, index. 1999. $18.

Allan J. Janssen
Constitutional Theology: Notes on the Book of Church Order *of the Reformed Church in America*
An absolutely indispensable aid to anyone responsible for the governance of the church, whether deacon, elder, minister, or denomination executive. Personnel and churches could be prevented from floundering, time in classes and synods could be saved, if only these guides for living together were followed, rather than approaching issues on an ad hoc basis. The wisdom of centuries has gone into this guide for governance. Janssen reaches beyond the pragmatic to show the underlying theology that governs our living in consistories, classes, and synods. Pp. xii, 321, index. 2000. $25.

Gregg A. Mast, editor
Raising the Dead, Sermons of Howard G. Hageman
Perhaps one of the most erudite and eloquent preachers of the latter half of the twentieth century, from his pulpit in the North Reformed Church in Newark Hageman was in demand as preacher and lecturer, as well as a professor of preaching, and later president, at New Brunswick Theological Seminary. Two series of sermons on Christ's seven last words open the book, followed by seven Christmas sermons, six for Easter, and four each for Ascension and Pentecost. While Hageman's eloquence was a gift improbable to teach or imitate, nonetheless these sermons will stimulate and excite all who care about great preaching. Pp. xxix, 241. 2000. $20.

James Hart Brumm, editor
Equipping the Saints, the Synod of New York, 1800-2000
The editor describes the convening of the Synod of New York, while Christopher Moore moves us from the early days in the mill to the present millennium. Betty L King describes the historic St. Thomas Reformed Church in the Virgin Islands, while Anna Melissa James describes the experience of black people in the Reformed Church in America. Scott Conrad and Stephen Hanson describe the different perspective of the northern reaches of the synod in the Classis of Mid-Hudson. Herman D. De Jong describes the changes in the Classis of Queens, while Michael Edwards offers practical perspectives on urban ministries. John E. Hiemstra describes the remarkable growth of the Asian church in the synod, while Russell L. Gasero offers a pictorial view. There is also a chronological list of congregations (which at one time ranged through New Jersey to Illinois to Oklahoma). Pp. xii, 185, illustrations, index. 2000. $16.

Joel R. Beeke, editor
Forerunner of the Great Awakening, sermons by Theodorus Jacobus Frelinghuysen, 1691-1747
The virile pietism of Frelinghuysen and his preaching seeking an experientially defined conversion is acknowledged as the beginning of the Great Awakening. An excellent introduction to Frelinghuysen is offered by Joel R. Beeke. Twenty-two sermons are included, intended to bring the hearer to an intimate awareness of sin and peril, through God's grace in conversion. The sermons offer an original source understanding of the Awakening. Pp. xliii, 339, 6 x 9". 2000. $28.

Russell L. Gasero
Historical Directory of the Reformed Church in America, 1628-2000
This newest edition of the historical directory contains the six thousand ordained ministers serving in over tweny thousand individual areas of service in more than seventeen hundred congregations. The listings of ministers, missionaries, and churches follows that of the directory of 1628-1992 (above). Pp. xvi, 720, 6 x 9". 2001. $70.

Eugene P. Heideman
From Mission to Church, The Reformed Church in America Mission to India
The story chronicles the period from the beginning of the mission under John Scudder in 1819 to 1987. Beginning with a focus on evangelism with the initiative in the hands of missionaries and mission societies, the organization of the Classis of Arcot puts the churches into relationship with the church in America. At the same time there is a growth of institutions in education and medicine. With the independence of India and the formation of the Church of South India in 1947, mission is seen as partnership, with the mission playing a supporting role to a self-determining church. The history is an honest portrayal of both failure and success. Pp. xix, 748, illustrations, maps, bibliography, index. 2001. $50.

Harry Boonstra
Our School: Calvin College and the Christian Reformed Church
Calvin College was indeed considered "our school" by members of the Christian Reformed Church. This sense of church ownership created strength and support but also the efforts of the church to impose its mores (and politics) upon both students and professors. Pp. xi, 155, bibliography, index. 2001. $15.

James I. Cook, ed.
The Church Speaks, Vol. 2, Papers of the Commission on Theology Reformed Church in America, 1985-2000
Includes "The Use of Scripture in Making Moral Decisions." Under "Church and Faith" are papers on liberation theology, the Nicene Creed, confirmation, conscience clauses, and the uniqueness of Christ. Under "Church and Sacraments" are considered children at the Lord's Table, while "Church and

Ministry" treats the role and authority of women in ministry, the laying on of hands in ordination, the commissioning of preaching elders, moral standards for church offices, and constitutional inquiries. Under "Church and Witness" are the relationship to Muslims and the farm crisis. "Church and Sexuality" considers homosexuality. Pp. xix, 315, appendix, scripture index, name index, subject index. 2002. $28.

John W. Coakley, editor
Concord Makes Strength, Essays in Reformed Ecumenism
Herman Harmelink III revisits the first volume in this series; Lynn Japinga describes our hesitant ecumenical history; Paul R. Fries discusses the theological roots of our ecumenical disposition; while Karl Blei gives a broader view of Reformed ecumenism. Areas of encounter concern full communion, Roman Catholic dialogue, the Joint Declaration on Justification, a Reformed-Catholic future, Reformed and evangelical and Eastern Orthodox, plus an attempt to see the future by Dale T. Irvin and Wesley Grandberg-Michaelson. Pp. xvii, 194, index. 2002. $19.

Robert P. Swierenga
Dutch Chicago, A History of Hollanders in the Windy City
From the very beginnings of Dutch immigration to Chicago, Swierenga traces the development primarily of Dutch Calvinists, but also of the smaller numbers of Jews and Roman Catholics. Of the former, their enclaves in the Groninger Hoek and Roseland, with further flight to the suburbs. The role of the church and Christian schools, as well as mutual aid societies, social clubs, truck farming, garbage and cartage, stores, services, and ethnic politics are covered in detail. Five appendices include garbage and cartage companies, churches, schools, missions, societies, clubs, and church membership. Pp. xx, 908, illustrations, maps, tables, bibliography, index, 6 x 9", hardcover, dust jacket. 2002. $49.

Paul L. Armerding
Doctors for the Kingdom, the work of the American Mission Hospital in the Kingdom of Saudi Arabia
Drawing upon original source materials from the missionary doctors and nurses involved, Armerding creates a compelling narrative of these men and women who witnessed to the love of Christ through the words and deeds of their medical mission. The book has been translated into Arabic and published by the King Abdulaziz Foundation in Riyadh, Saudi Arabia. The principal doctors cited in the book were featured in *Saudi Aramco World*, May/June 2004. Lavishly produced. Pp. 182, illustrations, glossary, gazetteer, maps, bibliography, 8 1/2 x 10 1/4, hardcover, dust jacket. 2003. $39.

Donald J. Bruggink & Kim N. Baker
By Grace Alone, Stories of the Reformed Church in America
Intended for the whole church. After a consideration of its European background in an introductory chapter "Reformed from What?," the story of the Dutch and their church in the New World from the early seventeenth

century to the present is told with attention paid to relationships to Native and African Americans at home and missions abroad. The movement of the church across the continent and immigration to Canada, as well as its ecumenical involvement, leads to a challenge for the future. Additional personal interest stories in sidebars, as well as time lines and resources; accompany each chapter. Pp. ix, 222, illustrations, index, 8 1/2 x 11". 2004. $29.

June Potter Durkee
Travels of an American Girl
Prior to WWII, June accompanied her parents on a trip through Europe to the Middle East and India. Her father, F. M. "Duke" Potter, was for thirty years a major force in mission policy and administration. The world and the missionaries, as seen through the eyes of a precocious ten year old who polished her account at age twelve, makes delightful and insightful reading. Pp. xv, 95, sketches, illustrations. 2004. $14.

Mary L. Kansfield
Letters to Hazel, Ministry within the Woman's Board of Foreign Missions of the Reformed Church in America
A collection of letters, written by overseas missionaries in appreciation of Hazel Gnade, who shepherded them through New York on their departures and returns, inspired this history of the Woman's Board. Kansfield chronicles how a concern for women abroad precipitated a nineteenth century "feminism" that in the cause of missions, took women out of their homes, gave them experience in organizational skills, fundraising and administration. Pp. xiii, 257, illustrations, appendices, bibliography, name index, subject index, 8 1/2 x 11". 2004. $29.

Johan Stellingwerff and Robert P. Swierenga, editors
Iowa Letters, Dutch Immigrants on the American Frontier
A collection of two hundred fifteen letters between settlers in Iowa and their family and friends in the Netherlands. Remarkable is the fact that the collection contains reciprocal letters covering a period of years. While few have heard of the Buddes and Wormsers, there are also letters between Hendrik Hospers, mayor of Pella and founder of Hospers, Iowa, and his father. Also unusual is that in contrast to the optimism of Hospers, there are the pessimistic letters of Andries N. Wormser, who complained that to succeed in American you had to "work like a German." Pp. xxvii, 701, illustrations, list of letters, bibliography, index, 6 x 9", hardcover, dust jacket. 2005. $49.

James C. Kennedy & Caroline J. Simon
Can Hope Endure: A Historical Case Study in Christian Higher Education
Hope was founded as a Christian college. How it has endured to the present without slipping either into secularism or a radical fundamentalism is the account of this book. The course has not always been steady, with factions within the school at times leaning either to the left or right. The account can perhaps be instructive in maintaining Hope's traditional centrist position. Pp. xvi, 249, bibliography, index, 6 x 9". 2005. $28.

Robert P. Swierenga
Dutch Chicago, A History of the Hollanders in the Windy City, second edition
Pp. xx, 908, illustrations, maps, tables, bibliography, index, 6 x 9", hardcover, dust jacket. 2005. $55.

LeRoy Koopman
Taking the Jesus Road, The Ministry of the Reformed Church in America among Native Americans
The ministry began in the seventeenth century, carried on by pastors who ministered to their Dutch congregants and native Americans. After the Revolutionary War, ministry moved from pastors to missionaries, increasing in activity following the Civil War. Koopman does not shy away from multiple failed government policies in which the church was often complicit, but he also records the steadfast devotion of both missionaries and lay workers who sought to bring assistance, love, and the gospel to native Americans. Pp. xiv, 512, illustrations, appendices including pastors, administrators, other personnel, and native American pastors, index, 6 x 9", hardcover, dust jacket. 2005. $49.